TWELVE SERMONS
ON
PRAYER

By
C. H. SPURGEON

BAKER BOOK HOUSE
Grand Rapids, Michigan

Reprinted by Baker Book House Company
First printing, January, 1971
Second printing, April, 1972

Standard Book Number: 8010-7923-3

Printed in the United States of America

CONTENTS

THE GOLDEN KEY OF PRAYER

A SERMON

Text.—"Call unto me, and I will answer thee, and shew thee great and mighty things, which thou knowest not."—Jeremiah xxxiii. 3.

SOME of the most learned works in the world smell of the midnight oil; but the most spiritual, and most comforting books and sayings of men usually have a savour about them of prison-damp. I might quote many instances: John Bunyan's *Pilgrim* may suffice instead of a hundred others; and this good text of ours, all mouldy and chill with the prison in which Jeremiah lay, hath nevertheless a brightness and a beauty about it, which it might never have had if it had not come as a cheering word to the prisoner of the Lord, shut up in the court of the prison-house. God's people have always in their worst condition found out the best of their God. He is good at all times; but he seemeth to be at His best when they are at their worst. Rutherford had a quaint saying, that when he was cast into the cellars of affliction, he remembered that the great King always kept his wine there, and he began to seek at once for the wine-bottles, and to drink of the "wines on the lees well refined." They who dive in the sea of affliction bring up rare pearls. You know, my companions in affliction, that it is so. You have proved that He is a faithful God, and that as your tribulations abound, so your consolations also abound by Christ Jesus.

My prayer is, in taking this text this morning that some other prisoners of the Lord may have its joyous promise spoken home to them; that you who are straitly shut up and cannot come forth by reason of present heaviness of spirit, may hear him say, as with a soft whisper in your ears, and in your hearts, "Call upon me, and I will answer thee, and shew thee great and mighty things which thou knowest not."

The text naturally splits itself up into three distinct particles of truth. Upon these let us speak as we are enabled by God the Holy Spirit. *First,* prayer commanded—"Call unto me"; *secondly,* an answer promised—"And I will answer thee"; *thirdly,* faith encouraged—"And shew thee great and mighty things which thou knowest not."

I. The first head is PRAYER COMMANDED.

We are not merely counselled and recommended to pray, but bidden to pray. This is great condescension. An hospital is

7

built: it is considered sufficient that free admission shall be given to the sick when they seek it; but no order in council is made that a man must enter its gates. A soup kitchen is well provided for in the depth of winter. Notice is promulgated that those who are poor may receive food on application; but no one thinks of passing an Act of Parliament, compelling the poor to come and wait at the door to take the charity. It is thought to be enough to proffer it without issuing any sort of mandate that men *shall* accept it. Yet so strange is *the infatuation of man* on the one hand, which makes him need a command to be merciful to his own soul, and so marvellous is the condescension of our gracious God on the other, that he issues a command of love without which not a man of Adam born would partake of the gospel feast, but would rather starve than come.

In the matter of prayer it is even so. God's own people need, or else they would not receive it, a command to pray. How is this? Because, dear friends, we are very subject to *fits of worldliness*, if indeed that be not our usual state. We do not forget to eat: we do not forget to take the shop shutters down: we do not forget to be diligent in business: we do not forget to go to our beds to rest: but we often do forget to wrestle with God in prayer, and to spend, as we ought to spend, long periods in consecrated fellowship with our Father and our God. With too many professors the ledger is so bulky that you cannot move it, and the Bible, representing their devotion, is so small that you might almost put it in your waistcoat pocket. Hours for the world! Moments for Christ! The world has the best, and our closet the parings of our time. We give our strength and freshness to the ways of mammon, and our fatigue and languor to the ways of God. Hence it is that we need to be commanded to attend to that very act which it ought to be our greatest happiness, as it is our highest privilege to perform, viz. to meet with our God. "Call upon me," saith He, for He knows that we are apt to forget to call upon God. "What meanest thou, oh, sleeper? arise and call upon thy God," is an exhortation which is needed by us as well as by Jonah in the storm.

He understands what *heavy hearts* we have sometimes, when under a sense of sin. Satan says to us, "Why should you pray? How can you hope to prevail? In vain, thou sayest, I will arise and go to my Father, for thou art not worthy to be one of his hired servants. How canst thou see the king's face after thou hast played the traitor against him? How wilt thou dare to approach unto the altar when thou hast thyself defiled it, and when the sacrifice which thou wouldst bring there is a poor polluted one?" O brethren, it is well for us that we are commanded to pray, or else in times of heaviness we might give it up. If God command me, unfit as I may be, I will creep to the footstool of grace; and since he says, "Pray without ceasing," though my words fail me and my heart itself will wander, yet I will still stammer out the wishes of my hungering soul and say, "O God, at least teach me to pray and help me to prevail with thee."

Are we not commanded to pray also because of our *frequent unbelief*! Unbelief whispers, "What profit is there if thou shouldst seek the Lord upon such-and-such a matter?" Either it is too trivial a matter, or it is too connected with temporals, or else it is a matter in which you have sinned too much, or else it is too high, too hard, too complicated a piece of business, you have no right to take that before God! So suggests the foul fiend of hell. Therefore, there stands written as an every-day precept suitable to every case into which a Christian can be cast, "Call unto me—call unto me." Art thou sick? Wouldst thou be healed? Cry unto me, for I am a Great Physician. Does providence trouble thee? Art thou fearful that thou shalt not provide things honest in the sight of man? Call unto me! Do thy children vex thee? Dost thou feel that which is sharper than un adder's tooth—a thankless child? Call unto me. Are thy griefs little yet painful, like small points and pricks of thorns? Call unto me! Is thy burden heavy as though it would make thy back break beneath its load? Call unto me! "Cast thy burden upon the Lord, and he shall sustain thee; he shall never suffer the righteous to be moved."

We must not leave our first part till we have made another remark. We ought to be very glad that God hath given us this command *in his word* that it may be sure and abiding. It may be a sensible exercise for some of you to find out how often in scripture you are told to pray. You will be surprised to find how many times such words as these are given; "Call upon me in the day of trouble, and I will deliver thee"—"Ye people, pour our your heart before him." "Seek ye the Lord while he may be found; call ye upon him while he is near." "Ask, and it shall be given you; seek, and ye shall find; knock, and it shall be opened unto you"—"Watch and pray, lest ye enter into temptation"—"Pray without ceasing"—"Come boldly unto the throne of grace," "Draw nigh to God and he will draw nigh to you." "Continue in prayer." I need not multiply where I could not possibly exhaust. I pick two or three out of this great bag of pearls. Come, Christian, you ought never to question whether you have a right to pray: you should never ask, "May I be permitted to come into His presence?" When you have so many commands, (and God's commands are all promises, and all enablings,) you may come boldly unto the throne of heavenly grace, by the new and living way through the rent veil.

But there are times when God not only commands His people to pray in the Bible, but He also commands them to pray directly *by the motions of His Holy Spirit.* You who know the inner life comprehend me at once. You feel on a sudden, possibly in the midst of business, the pressing thought that you *must* retire to pray. It may be, you do not at first take particular notice of the inclination, but it comes again, and again, and again— "Retire and pray!" I find that in the matter of prayer, I am myself very much like a water-wheel which runs well when there is plenty of water, but which turns with very little force when the brook is growing shallow; or, like the ship which flies over the waves, putting out all her canvas when the wind is favourable, but which has to tack about most laboriously when there is but little of the favouring breeze. Now, it strikes me that whenever our Lord gives you the special inclination to pray, that you should double your dilligence. You ought always to pray and not to faint, yet when He gives you the special longing after prayer, and you feel a peculiar aptness and enjoyment in it, you have, over and above the command which is constantly binding, another command which should compel you to cheerful obedience. At such times I think we may stand in the position of David, to whom the Lord said, "When thou hearest a sound of a going in the tops of the mulberry trees, then shalt thou bestir thyself." That going in the tops of the mulberry trees may have been the footfalls of angels hastening to the help of David, and then David was to smite the Philistines, and when God's mercies are coming, their footfalls are our desires to pray; and our desires to pray should be at once an indication that the set time to favour Zion is come. Sow plentifully now, for thou canst sow in hope; plough joyously now, for thy harvest is sure. Wrestle now, Jacob, for thou are about to be made a prevailing prince, and thy name shall be called Israel. Now is thy time, spiritual merchantmen; the market is high, trade much; thy profit shall be large. See to it that thou usest right well the golden hour, and reap thy harvest whilst the sun shines.

II. Let us now take the second head—AN ANSWER PROMISED.

We ought not to tolerate for a minute the ghastly and grievous thought that God will not answer prayer. *His nature,* as manifested in Christ Jesus, demands it. He has revealed Himself in the gospel, as a God of love, full of grace and truth; and how can He refuse to help those of His creatures who humbly in His own appointed way seek His face and favour?

When the Athenian senate, upon one occasion, found it most convenient to meet together in the open air, as they were sitting in their deliberations, a sparrow, pursued by a hawk, flew in the direction of the senate. Being hard pressed by the bird of prey, it sought shelter in the bosom·of one of the senators. He, being a man of rough and vulgar mould, took the bird from his bosom, dashed it on the ground and so killed it. Whereupon the whole senate rose in uproar, and without one single dissenting voice, condemned him to die, as being unworthy of a seat in the senate with them or to be called an Athenian, if he did not render succour to a creature that confided in him. Can we suppose that the God of heaven, whose nature is love, could tear out of His bosom the poor fluttering dove that flies from the eagle of justice into the bosom of His mercy? Will He give the invitation to us to seek His face, and when we, as He knows, with so much trepidation of fear, yet summon courage enough to fly into His bosom, will He then be unjust and ungracious enough to forget to hear our cry and to answer us? Let us not think so hardly of the God of heaven.

Let us recollect next, *His past character* as well as His nature. I mean the character which He has won for Himself by His past deeds of grace. Consider, my brethren, that one stupendous display of bounty—if I were to mention a thousand I could not give a better illustration of the character of God than that one deed—"He that spared not his own Son, but freely delivered him up for us all"—and it is not my inference only, but the inspired conclusion of an apostle—"how shall he not with him also freely give us all things?" If the Lord did not refuse to listen to my voice when I was a guilty sinner and an enemy, how can He disregard my cry now, that I am justified and saved! How is it that He heard the voice of my misery when my heart knew it not, and would not seek relief, if after all He will not hear me now that I am His child, His friend? The streaming wounds of Jesus are the sure guarantee for answered prayer. George Herbert represents in that quaint poem of his," *The Bag,*"the Saviour saying—

> "If ye have anything to send or write
> (I have no bag, but here is room)
> Unto my Father's hands and sight,
> (Believe me) it shall safely come.
> That I shall mind what you impart
>
> Look, you may put it very near my heart,
> Or if hereafter any of friends
> Will use me in this kind, the door
> Shall still be open; what he sends
> I will present and somewhat more
> Not to his hurt."

Surely George Herbert's thought was that the atonement was in itself a guarantee that prayer must be heard, that the great gash made near the Saviour's heart, which let the light into the very depths of the heart of Deity, was a proof that He who sits in heaven would hear the cry of His people. You misread Calvary, if you think that prayer is useless.

But, beloved, we have *The Lord's own promise* for it, and He is a God that cannot lie. "Call upon me in the day of trouble and I will answer thee." Has He not said, "Whatsoever ye shall ask in prayer, believe that ye shall have it and ye shall have it." We cannot pray, indeed, unless we believe this doctrine; "for he that cometh to God must believe that he is, and that he is the rewarder of them that diligently seek him"; and if we have any question at all about whether our prayer will be heard, we are comparable to him that wavereth; "for he who wavereth is like a wave of the sea, driven with the wind and tossed; let not that man think that he shall receive anything of the Lord."

Furthermore, it is not necessary, still it may strengthen the point, if we added that *our own experience* leads us to believe that God will answer prayer. I must not speak for you; but I may speak for myself. If there be anything I know, anything that I am quite assured of beyond all question, it is that praying breath is never spent in vain. If no other man here can say it, I dare to say it, and I know that I can prove it. My own conversion is the result of prayer, long, affectionate, earnest, importunate. Parents prayed for me; God heard their cries, and here I am to preach the Gospel. Since then I have adventured upon some things that were far beyond my capacity as I thought; but I have never failed, because I have cast myself upon the Lord.

You know as a church that I have not scrupled to indulge large ideas of what we might do for God; and we have accomplished all that we purposed. I have sought God's aid, and assistance, and help, in all my manifold undertakings, and though I cannot tell here the story of my private life in God's work, yet if it were written it would be a standing proof that there is a God that answers prayer. He has heard *my* prayers, not now and then, nor once nor twice, but so many times, that it has grown into a habit with me to spread my case before God with the absolute certainty that whatsoever I ask of God, He will give to me. It is not now a "Perhaps" or a possibility. I know that my Lord answers me, and I dare not doubt, it were indeed folly if I did. As I am sure that a certain amount of leverage will lift a weight, so I know that a certain amount of prayer will get anything from God. As the rain-cloud brings the shower, so prayer brings the blessing. As spring scatters flowers, so supplication ensures mercies. In all labour there is profit, but most of all in the work of intercession: I am sure of this, for I have reaped it.

Still remember that prayer is always to be offered in submission to God's will; that when we say, God heareth prayer, we do not intend by that, that He always gives us literally what we ask for. We do mean, however, this, that He gives us what is best for us; and that if He does not give us the mercy we ask for in silver, He bestows it upon us in gold. If He doth not take away the thorn in the flesh, yet He saith, "My grace is sufficient for thee," and that comes to the same in the end.

Lord Bolingbroke said to the Countess of Huntingdon, "I cannot understand, your ladyship, how you can make out earnest prayer to be consistent with submission to the divine will." "My lord," said she, "that is a matter of no difficulty. If I were a courtier of some generous king, and he gave me permission to ask any favour I pleased of him, I should be sure to put it thus, 'Will your majesty be graciously pleased to grant me such-and-such a favour; but at the same time though I very much desire it, if it would in any way detract from your majesty's honour, or if in your majesty's judgment it should seem better that I did not have this favour, I shall be quite as content to go without it as to receive it.' So you see I might earnestly offer a petition, and yet I might submissively leave it in the king's hands." So with God. We never offer up prayer without inserting that clause, either in spirit or in words, "Nevertheless, not as I will, but as thou wilt; not my will but thine be done." We can only pray without an "if" when we are quite sure that our will must be God's will, because God's will is fully our will.

III. I come to our third point, which I think is full of encouragement to all those who exercise the hallowed art of prayer; ENCOURAGEMENT TO FAITH. "I will shew thee great and mighty things which thou knowest not."

Let us just remark that this was originally spoken to a prophet in prison; and, therefore, it applies in the first place to *every teacher*; and, indeed, as every teacher must be a learner, it has a bearing upon *every learner* in divine truth. The best way by which a prophet and teacher and learner can know the reserved truths, the higher and more mysterious truths of God, is by waiting upon God in prayer. I noticed very specially yesterday in reading the Book of the Prophet Daniel, how Daniel found out Nebuchadnezzar's dream. The soothsayers, the magicians, the astrologers, of the Chaldees brought out their curious books and

B

their strange-looking instruments, and began to mutter their *abracadabra* and all sorts of mysterious incantations, but they all failed. What did Daniel do? He set himself to prayer, and knowing that the prayer of a united body of men has more prevalence than the prayer of one, we find that Daniel called together his brethren, and bade them unite with him in earnest prayer that God would be pleased of His infinite mercy to open up the vision. And in the case of John, who was the Daniel of the New Testament, you remember he saw a book in the right hand of Him who sat on the throne—a book sealed with seven seals which none was found worthy to open or to look thereon. What did John do? The book was by-and-by opened by the Lion of the Tribe of Judah, who had prevailed to open the book; but it is written first before the book was opened, "I wept much." Yes, and the tears of John which were his liquid prayers, were, as far as he was concerned, the sacred keys by which the folded book was opened.

Brethren in the ministry, you who are teachers in the Sabbath school, and all of you who are learners in the college of Christ Jesus, I pray you remember that prayer is your best means of study; like Daniel you shall understand the dream, and the interpretation thereof, when you have sought unto God; and like John you shall see the seven seals of precious truth unloosed, after that you have wept much. "Yea, if thou criest after knowledge, and liftest up the voice for understanding; if thou seekest her as silver, and searchest for her as for hid treasures; then shalt thou understand the fear of the Lord and find the knowledge of God." Stones are not broken, except by an earnest use of the hammer; and the stone-breaker usually goes down on his knees. Use the hammer of vengeance, too, and let the knee of prayer be exercised, too, and there is not a stony doctrine in Revelation which is useful for you to understand, which will not fly into shivers under the exercise of prayer and faith. "*Bene orasse est bene studuisse*" was a wise sentence of Luther, which has been so often quoted, that we hardly venture but to hint at it. "To have prayed well is to have studied well." You may force your way through anything with the leverage of prayers. Thoughts and reasonings may be like the steel wedges which may open a way into truth; but prayer is the lever, the prise which forces open the iron chest of sacred mystery, that we may get the treasure that is hidden therein for those who can force their way to reach it. The kingdom of heaven still suffereth violence, and the violent taketh it by force. Take care that ye work away with the mighty implement of prayer, and nothing can stand against you.

We must not, however, stop there. We have applied the text

to only one case; it is applicable to a hundred. We single out another. _The saint may expect to discover deeper experience_ and to know more of the higher spiritual life, by being much in prayer. There are different translations of my text. One version renders it, "I will shew thee great and fortified things which thou knowest not." Another reads it, "Great and reserved things which thou knowest not." Now, all the developments of spiritual life are not alike easy of attainment. There are the common frames and feelings of repentance, and faith, and joy, and hope, which are enjoyed by the entire family: but there is an upper realm of rapture, of communion, and conscious union with Christ, which is far from being the common dwelling-place of believers. All believers see Christ; but all believers do not put their fingers into the prints of the nails, nor thrust their hand into His side. We have not all the high privilege of John to lean upon Jesus' bosom, nor of Paul, to be caught up into the third heaven.

In the ark of salvation we find a lower, second, and third storey; all are in the ark, but all are not in the same storey. Most Christians, as to the river of experience, are only up to the ankles; some others have waded till the stream is up to the knees: a few find it breast-high; and but a few—oh! how few!—find it a river to swim in, the bottom of which they cannot touch. My brethren, there are heights in experimental knowledge of the things of God which the eagle's eye of acumen and philosophic thought have never seen; and there are secret paths which the lion's whelp of reason and judgment hath not as yet learned to travel. God alone can bear us there; but the chariot in which He takes us up, and the fiery steeds with which that chariot is dragged, are prevailing prayers. Prevailing prayer is victorious over the God of mercy. "By his strength he had power with God: yea, he had power over the angel, and prevailed: he wept, and made supplication unto him: he found him in Beth-el, and there he spake with us." Prevailing prayer takes the Christian to Carmel, and enables him to cover heaven with clouds of blessing, and earth with floods of mercy. Prevailing prayer bears the Christian aloft to Pisgah and shows him the inheritance reserved; ay, and it elevates him to Tabor and transfigures him, till in the likeness of his Lord, as he is, so are we also in this world. If you would reach to something higher than ordinary grovelling experience, look to the Rock that is higher than you, and look with the eye of faith through the windows of importunate prayer. To grow in experience then, there must be much prayer.

You must have patience with me while I apply this text to two or three more cases. It is certainly true of _the sufferer under trial :_ if he waits upon God in prayer much he shall receive greater deliverances than he has ever dreamed of—"great and mighty things which thou knowest not." Here is Jeremiah's testimony:—"Thou drewest near in the day that I called upon thee: thou saidst, Fear not. O Lord, thou hast pleaded the causes of my soul; thou hast redeemed my life." And David's is the same:—"I called upon the Lord in distress: the Lord answered me, and set me in a large place. . . . I will praise thee: for thou hast heard me, and art become my salvation." And yet again:—"Then they cried unto the Lord in their trouble, and He delivered them out of their distresses. And He led them forth by the right way, that they might go to a city of habitation." "My husband is dead," said the poor woman, "and my creditor is come to take my two sons as bondsmen." She hoped that Elijah would possibly say, "What are your debts? I will pay them." Instead of that, he multiplies her oil till it is written, "Go thou and pay thy debts, and"—what was the "and"?—"live thou and thy children upon the rest." So often it will happen that God will not only help His people through the miry places of the way, so that they may just stand on the other side of the slough, but He will bring them safely far on the journey.

That was a remarkable miracle, when in the midst of the storm, Jesus Christ came walking upon the sea, the disciples received Him into the ship, and not only was the sea calm, but it is recorded, "Immediately the ship was at the land whither they went." That was a mercy over and above what they asked. I sometimes hear you pray and make use of a quotation which is not in the Bible:—"He is able to do exceeding abundantly above what we *can* ask or even think." It is not so written in the Bible. I do not, know what we can ask or what we can think. But it is said, "He is able to do exceeding abundantly above what we ask or even think." Let us then, dear friends, when we are in great trial only say, "Now I am in prison; like Jeremiah, I will pray as he did, for I have God's command to do it; and I will look out as he did, expecting that He will show me reserved mercies which I know nothing of at present." He will not merely bring His people through the battle, covering their heads in it, but He will bring them forth with banners waving, to divide the spoil with the mighty, and to claim their portion with the strong. Expect great things of a God who gives such great promises as these.

Again, *here is encouragement for the worker*. My dear friends, wait upon God much in prayer, and you have the promise that He will do greater things for you than you know of. We know not how much capacity for usefulness there may be in us. That ass's jaw-bone lying there upon the earth, what can it do?

Nobody knows what it can do. It gets into Samson's hands, what can it *not* do? No one knows what it cannot do now that a Samson wields it. And you, friend, have often thought yourself to be as contemptible as that bone, and you have said, "What can I do?" Ay, but when Christ by His Spirit grips you, what can you not do? Truly you may adopt Paul's language and say, "I can do all things through Christ who strengtheneth me."

However, do not depend upon prayer without effort. In a certain school there was one girl who knew the Lord, a very gracious, simple-hearted, trustful child. As usual, grace developed itself in the child according to the child's position. Her lessons were always best said of any in the class. Another girl said to her, "How is it that your lessons are always so well said?" "I pray God to help me," she said, "to learn my lesson." "Well," thought the other, "Then I will do the same." The next morning when she stood up in the class she knew nothing; and when she was in disgrace she complained to the other, "Why I prayed God to help me learn my lesson and I do not know anything of it. What is the use of prayer?" "But did you sit down and try to learn it?" "Oh, no," she said, "I never looked at the book." "Ah," then said the other, "I asked God to help me to learn my lesson; but I then sat down to it studiously, and I kept at it till I knew it well, and I learned it easily, because my earnest desire, which I had expressed to God, was, help me to be diligent in endeavouring to do my duty."

So is it with some who come up to prayer-meetings and pray, and then they fold their arms and go away hoping that God's work will go on. Like the negro woman singing, "Fly abroad, thou mighty gospel," but not putting a penny in the plate; so that her friend touched her and said, "But how can it fly if you don't give it wings to fly with?" There be many who appear to be very mighty in prayer, wondrous in supplications; but then they require God to do what they can do themselves, and, therefore, God does nothing at all for them. "I shall leave my camel untied," said an Arab once to Mahomet, "and trust to providence." "Tie it up tight," said Mahomet, "and then trust to providence."

So you that say, "I shall pray and trust my Church, or my class, or my work to God's goodness," may rather hear the voice of experience and wisdom which says, "Do thy best; work as if all rested upon thy toil; as if thy own arm would bring thy salvation"; "and when thou hast done all, cast thyself on him without whom it is in vain to rise up early and to sit up late, and to eat the bread of carefulness; and if he speed thee give him the praise."

I shall not detain you many minutes longer, but I want to notice that this promise ought to prove useful for the comforting of those who are intercessors for others. You who are calling upon God to save your children, to bless your neighbours, to remember your husbands or your wives in mercy, may take comfort from this, "I will shew thee great and mighty things, which thou knowest not."

A celebrated minister in the last century, one Mr. Bailey, was the child of a godly mother. This mother had almost ceased to pray for her husband, who was a man of a most ungodly stamp, and a bitter persecutor. The mother prayed for her boy, and while he was yet eleven or twelve years of age, eternal mercy met with him. So sweetly instructed was the child in the things of the kingdom of God, that the mother requested him—and for some time he always did so—to conduct family prayer in the house. Morning and evening this little one laid open the Bible; and though the father would not deign to stop for the family prayer, yet on one occasion he was rather curious to know "what sort of an out the boy would make of it," so he stopped on the other side of the door, and God blessed the prayer of his own child under thirteen years of age to his conversion. The mother might well have read my text with streaming eyes, and said, "Yes, Lord, thou hast shewn me great and mighty things which I knew not: thou hast not only saved my boy, but through my boy thou hast brought my husband to the truth."

You cannot guess how greatly God will bless you. Only go and stand at His door, you cannot tell what is in reserve for you. If you do not beg at all, you will get nothing; but if you beg He may not only give you, as it were, the bones and broken meat, but He may say to the servant at His table, "Take thou that dainty meat, and set that before the poor man." Ruth went to glean; she expected to get a few good ears: but Boaz said, "Let her glean even among the sheaves, and rebuke her not"; he said moreover to her, "At meal-time come thou hither, and eat of the bread, and dip thy morsel in the vinegar." Nay, she found a husband where she only expected to find a handful of barley. So in prayer for others, God may give us such mercies that we shall be astounded at them, since we expected but little. Hear what is said of Job, and learn its lesson, "And the Lord said, My servant Job shall pray for you: for him will I accept: lest I deal with you after your folly, in that ye have not spoken of me the thing which is right, like my servant Job. . . . And the Lord turned the captivity of Job, when he prayed for his friends: also the Lord gave Job twice as much as he had before."

Now, this word to close with. Some of you are seekers for your own conversion. God has quickened you to solemn prayer about your own souls. You are not content to go to hell, you want heaven; you want washing in the precious blood; you want eternal life. Dear friends, I pray take you this text—God himself speaks it to you—"Call unto me, and I will answer thee, and shew thee great and mighty things, which thou knowest not." At once take God at His word. Get home, go into your chamber and shut the door, and try Him. Young man, I say, try the Lord. Young woman, prove Him, see whether He be true or not. If God be true, you cannot seek mercy at His hands through Jesus Christ and get a negative reply. He must, for His own promise and character bind Him to it, open mercy's gate to you who knock with all your heart. God help you, believing in Christ Jesus, to cry aloud unto God, and His answer of peace is already on the way to meet you. You shall hear Him say, "Your sins which are many are all forgiven."

The Lord bless you for His love's sake. Amen.

THE RAVEN'S CRY

A Sermon

Text.—"He giveth to the beast his food, and to the young ravens which cry."—Ps. cxlvii. 9.

I SHALL open this sermon with a quotation. I must give you in Caryl's own words his note upon ravens. "Naturalists tell us, that when the raven hath fed his young in the nest till they are well fledged and able to fly abroad, then he thrusts them out of the nest, and will not let them abide there, but puts them to get their own living. Now when these young ones are upon their first flight from their nest, and are little acquainted with means how to help themselves with food, then the Lord provides food for them. It is said by credible authorities, that the raven is marvellous strict and severe in this; for as soon as his young ones are able to provide for themselves, he will not fetch any more food for them; yea, some affirm, the old ones will not suffer them to stay in the same country where they were bred; and if so, then they must needs wander. We say proverbially, 'Need makes the old wife trot'; we may say, and 'the young ones too.' It hath been, and possibly is, the practice of some parents towards their children, who, as soon as they can shift for themselves, and are fit in any competency to get their bread, they turn them out of doors, as the raven doth his young ones out of the nest. Now, saith the Lord in the text, when the young ones of the raven are at this pinch, that they are turned off, and wander for lack of meat, who then provides for them? do not I, the Lord? do not I, who provide for the old raven, provide for his young ones, both while they abide in the nest and when they wander for lack of meat?"

Solomon sent the sluggard to the ant, and learned himself lessons from conies, greyhounds, and spiders: let us be willing to be instructed by any of God's creatures, and go to the ravens' nest to-night to learn as in a school.

Our blessed Lord once derived a very potent argument from ravens—an argument intended to comfort and cheer those of His servants who were oppressed with needless anxieties about their temporal circumstances. To such He said, "Consider the ravens: for they neither sow nor reap; which neither have store-house nor barn; and God feedeth them: how much more are ye better than the fowls?"

Following the Master's logic I shall argue to-night on this wise:

20

Consider the ravens as they cry; with harsh, inarticulate, croaking notes they make known their wants, and your heavenly Father answers their prayer and sends them food; you, too, have begun to pray and to seek His favour; are ye not much better than they? Doth God care for ravens, and will He not care for you? Doth He hearken to the cries of the unfledged ravens in their nests, when hungry they cry unto Him and watch to be fed? Doth He, I say, supply them in answer to their cries, and will He not answer you, poor trembling children of men who are seeking His face and favour through Jesus Christ? The whole business of this evening will be just simply to work that one thought out. I shall aim to-night, under the guidance of the Holy Spirit, to say something to those who have been praying for mercy, but as yet have not received it; who have gone on their knees, perhaps for months, with one exceeding great and bitter cry, but as yet know not the way of peace. Their sin still hangs like a millstone about their neck; they sit in the valley of the shadow of death; no light has dawned upon them, and they are wringing their hands and moaning, "Hath God forgotten to be gracious? Hath He shut His ear against the prayers of seeking souls? Will He be mindful of sinners' piteous cries no more? Shall penitents' tears drop upon the earth, and no longer move His compassion?" Satan, too, is telling you, dear friends, who are now in this state of mind, that God will never hear you, that He will let you cry till you die, that you shall pant out your life in sighs and tears, and that at the end you shall be cast into the lake of fire. I long to-night to give you some comfort and encouragement. I want to urge you to cry yet more vehemently; to come to the cross and lay hold of it, and vow that you will never leave its shadow till you find the boon which your soul covets. I want to move you, if God the Holy Ghost shall help me, so that you will say within yourselves, like Queen Esther, "I will go in unto the King, and if I perish, I perish"; and may you add to that the vow of Jacob, "I will not let thee go, except thou bless me!"

Here, then, is the question in hand: GOD HEARS THE YOUNG RAVENS; WILL HE NOT HEAR YOU?

I. I argue that He will, first, when I remember that *it is only a raven that cries, and that you, in some senses, are much better than a raven.* The raven is but a poor unclean bird, whose instant death would make no sort of grievous gap in creation. If thousands of ravens had their necks wrung to-morrow, I do not know that there would be any vehement grief and sorrow in the universe about them; it would simply be a number of poor birds dead, and that would be all. *But you are an immortal soul.* The raven is gone when life is over, there is no raven any longer; but when your present life is past, you have not ceased to be; you are but launched upon the sea of life; you have but begun to live for ever. You will see earth's hoary mountains crumble to nothingness before your immortal spirit shall expire; the moon shall have paled her feeble light, and the sun's more mighty fires shall have been quenched in perpetual darkness, and yet your spirit shall still be marching on in its everlasting course—an everlasting course of misery, unless God hears your cry.

> "Oh, that truth immense,
> This mortal, immortality shall wear!
> The pulse of mind shall never cease to play;
> By God awakened, it for ever throbs,
> Eternal as His own eternity!
> Above the angels, or below the fields:
> To mount in glory, or in shame descend—
> Mankind are destined by resistless doom."

Do you think, then, that God will hear the poor bird that is and is not, and is here a moment and is blotted out of existence, and will He not hear you, an immortal soul, whose duration is to be co-equal with His own? I think it surely must strike you that if He hears the dying raven He will also hear an undying man.

Moreover, I never heard of ravens that they were made in the image of God; but I do find that, defiled, deformed, and debased as our race is, yet originally God said, "Let us make man in our own image." There is something about man which is not to be found in the lower creatures, the best and noblest of whom are immeasurably beneath the meanest child of Adam. There is a dignity about the fact of manhood which is not to be found in all the beasts of the field, be they which they may. Behemoth and Leviathan are put in subjection beneath the foot of man. The eagle cannot soar so high as his soul mounteth, nor the lion feed on such royal meat as his spirit hungereth after. And dost thou think that God will hear so low and so mean a creature as a raven and yet not hear thee, when *thou art one of the race that was formed in His own image ?* Oh! think not so hardly and so foolishly of Him Whose ways are always equal! I will put this to yourselves. Does not nature itself teach that man is to be cared for above the fowls of the air? If you heard the cries of young ravens, you might feel compassion enough for those birds to give them food if you knew how to feed them; but I cannot believe that any of you would succour the birds, and yet would not fly upon the wings of compassion to the rescue of a perishing infant whose cries you might hear from the place where it was cast by cruel neglect. If, in the stillness of the night, you heard the plaintive cry of a man expiring in sickness, unpitied in the streets, would you not arise and help him? I am sure you would if you are one who would help a raven. If you have any compassion for a raven, much more would you have pity upon a man. And do you not think that God, the All-wise One, when He cares for these unfledged birds in the nest, will be sure also to care for you? Your heart says, "Yes"; then henceforth answer the unbelief of your heart by turning its own just reasoning against it.

But I hear you say, "Ah! but the raven is not sinful as I am; it may be an unclean bird, but it cannot be so unclean as I am morally, it may be black in hue, but I am black with sin; a raven cannot break the Sabbath, cannot swear, cannot commit adultery; a raven cannot be a drunkard; it cannot defile itself with vices such as those with which I am polluted." I know all that, friend, and it may seem to you to make your case more hopeless; but I do not think it does so really. Just think of it for a minute. What does this prove? Why, *that you are a creature capable of sinning, and, consequently, that you are an intelligent spirit living in a sense in which a raven does not live.* You are a creature moving in the spirit-world; you belong to the world of souls, in which the raven has no portion. The raven cannot sin, because it has no spirit, no soul; but you are an intelligent agent, of which the better part is your soul. Oh, if you will but think of it, you must see that it is not possible for a raven's cry to gain an audience of the ear of divine benevolence, and yet for your prayer to be despised and disregarded by the Most High.

> " The insect that with puny wing,
> Just shoots along one summer's ray;
> The flow'ret, which the breath of Spring
> Wakes into life for half a day;
> The smallest mote, the tenderest hair,
> All feel our heavenly Father's care."

Surely, then, He will have respect unto the cry of the humble, and will not refuse their prayer. I can hardly leave this point without remarking that the mention of a raven should encourage a sinner. As an old author writes, "Among fowls He doth not mention the hawk or falcon, which are highly prized and fed by princes; nor the sweet singing nightingale, or such like musical pretty birds, which men keep choicely and much delight in; but He chooses that hateful and malicious bird the croaking raven, whom no man values but as she eats up the carrion which might annoy him. Behold then, and wonder at the providence and kindness of God, that He should provide food for the raven, a creature of so dismal a hue, and of so untuneable a tone, a creature that is so odious to most men, and ominous to some. There is a great providence of God seen in providing for the ant, who gathers her meat in summer; but a greater in the raven, who, though he forgets, or is careless to provide for himself, yet God provides and layeth up for him. One would think the Lord should say of ravens, Let them shift for themselves or perish; no, the Lord God doth not despise any work of His hands; the raven hath his being from God, and therefore the raven shall be provided for by Him; not only the fair innocent dove, but the ugly raven hath his meat from God. Which clearly shows that the want of excellence in thee, thou black, raven-like sinner, will not prevent thy cry from being heard in heaven. Unworthiness the blood of Jesus shall remove, and defilement He shall utterly cleanse away. Only believe on Jesus, and thou shalt find peace.

II. Then, in the next place, *there is a great deal of difference between your cry and the cry of a raven.* When the young ravens cry, I suppose they scarcely know what they want. They have a natural instinct which makes them cry for food, but their cry does not in itself express their want. You would soon find out, I suppose, that they meant food; but they have no articulate speech; they do not utter so much as a single word; it is just a constant, croaking, craving cry, and that is all. But *you* do know what you want, and few as your words are, your heart knows its own bitterness and dire distress. Your sighs and groans have an obvious meaning; your understanding is at the right hand of your necessitous heart. You know that you want peace and pardon; you know that you need Jesus, His precious blood, His perfect righteousness. Now, if God hears such a strange, chattering, indistinct cry as that of a raven, do you not think that He will also hear the rational and expressive prayer of a poor, needy, guilty soul who is crying unto Him, "God be merciful to me a sinner"? Surely your reason tells you that!

Moreover, *the young ravens cannot use arguments, for they have no understanding.* They cannot say as you can—

> " He knows what arguments I'd take
> To wrestle with my God,
> I'd plead for his own mercy's sake,
> And for a Saviour's blood."

They have one argument, namely, their dire necessity, which forces their cry from them, but beyond this they cannot go; and even this they cannot set forth in order, or describe in language. But you have a multitude of arguments ready to hand, and you have an understanding with which to set them in array and marshal them to besiege the throne of grace. Surely, if the mere plea of the unuttered want of the raven prevails with God, much more shall you prevail with the Most High if you can argue your case before Him, and come unto Him with arguments in your mouth. Come, thou despairing one, and try my Lord! I do beseech thee now let that doleful ditty ascend into the ears of mercy! Open that bursting heart and let it out in tears, if words are beyond thy power.

A raven, however, I fear, has sometimes a great advantage over some sinners who seek God in prayer, namely in this: *young ravens are more in earnest about their food than some are about their souls.* This, however, is no discouragement to you, but rather a reason why you should be more earnest than you have hitherto been. When ravens want food, they do not cease crying till they have got it: there is no quieting a hungry young raven till his mouth is full, and there is no quieting a sinner when he is really in earnest till he gets his heart full of divine mercy. I would that some of you prayed more vehemently! "The kingdom of heaven suffereth violence, and the violent take it by force." An old Puritan said, "Prayer is a cannon set at the gate of heaven to burst open its gates": you must take the city by storm if you would have it. You will not ride to heaven on a feather-bed, you must go on pilgrimage; there is no going to the land of glory while you are sound asleep, dreamy sluggards will have to wake up in hell. If God has made you to feel in your soul the need of salvation, cry like one who is awake and alive; be in earnest; cry aloud; spare not; and then I think you will find that if He hears such a cry as the raven's, it is much more certain that He will hear yours.

III. Remember, that *the matter of your prayer is more congenial to the ear of God than the raven's cry for meat. All that the young ravens cry for is food* ; give them a little carrion and they have done. Your cry must be much more pleasing to God's ear, for you entreat for forgiveness through the blood of His dear Son. It is a nobler occupation for the Most High to be bestowing spiritual than natural gifts. The streams of grace flow from the upper springs. I know He is so condescending that He does not dishonour Himself even when He drops food into the young raven's mouth; but still, there is more dignity about the work of giving peace, and pardon, and reconciliation to the sons of men. Eternal love appointed a way of mercy from before the foundation of the world, and infinite wisdom is engaged with boundless power to carry out the divine design; surely the Lord must take much pleasure in saving the sons of men. If God is pleased to supply the beast of the field, do you not think that He delights much more to supply His own child? I think you would find more congenial employment in teaching your own children than you would in merely foddering your ox, or scattering barley among the fowls at the barn door; because there would be in the first work something nobler, which would more fully call up all your powers and bring out your inward self. I am not left here to conjecture. It is written, "He delighteth in mercy." When God uses His power He cannot be sad, for He is a happy God; but if there be such a thing possible as the Infinite Deity being more happy at one time than at another, it is when He is forgiving sinners through the precious blood of Jesus.

Ah! sinner, when you cry to God you give Him an opportunity to do that which He loves most to do, for He delights to forgive, to press His Ephraim to His bosom, to say of His prodigal son, "He was lost, but is found; he was dead, but is alive again." This is more comfortable to the Father's heart than the feeding of the fatted calf, or tending the cattle of a thousand hills. Since then, dear friends, you are asking for something which it will honour God far more to give than the mere gift of food to ravens, I think there comes a very forcible blow of my argumentative hammer to-night to break your unbelief in pieces. May God the Holy Ghost, the true Comforter, work in you mightily! Surely the God Who gives food to ravens will not deny peace and pardon to seeking sinners. Try Him! Try Him at this moment! Nay, stir not! Try Him *now*.

IV. We must not pause on any one point when the whole subject is so prolific. There is another source of comfort, for you, namely, that *the ravens are nowhere commanded to cry. When they cry their petition is unwarranted by any specific exhortation from the Divine mouth, while you have a warrant derived from Divine exhortations to approach the throne of God in prayer.* If a rich man should open his house to those who were *not* invited he would surely receive those who *were* invited. Ravens come without being bidden, yet they are not sent away empty; you come as a bidden and an invited guest; how shall you be denied? Do you think you are not bidden? Listen to this: "*Whosoever* calleth on the name of the Lord shall be saved." "Call upon me in the day of trouble, and I will deliver thee, and thou shalt glorify me." "Go ye into all the world, and preach the gospel *to every creature ;* he that believeth and is baptized shall be saved; he that believeth not shall be damned." "Believe in the Lord Jesus Christ, and thou shalt be saved." "Repent and be baptized, every one of you, in the name of the Lord Jesus."

These are exhortations given without any limitation as to character. They freely invite you; nay, they bid you come. Oh! after this can you think that God will spurn you? The window is open, the raven flies in, and the God of mercy does not chase it out; the door is open, and the word of promise bids you come; think not that He will give you a denial, but believe rather that He will "receive you graciously and love you freely," and then you shall "render to him the calves of your lips." At any rate try Him! Try Him even now!

V. Again, there is yet another and a far mightier argument. *The cry of a young raven is nothing but the natural cry of a creature, but your cry, if it be sincere, is the result of a work of grace in your heart.* When the raven cries to heaven it is nothing but the raven's own self that cries; but when *you* cry "God be merciful to me a sinner,"—it is God the Holy Spirit crying in you. It is the new life which God has given you crying to the source from whence it came to have farther communion and communication in sincerity and in truth. We can, if we think it right, teach our children to "say their prayers," but we cannot teach them to "pray." You may make a "prayer-book," but you cannot put a grain of "prayer" into a book, for it is too spiritual a matter to be encased between leaves. Some of you, perhaps, may "read prayers" in the family; I will not denounce the practice, but I will say this much of it—you may read those "prayers" for seventy years, and yet you may never once pray, for prayer is quite a different thing from mere words. True prayer is the trading of the heart with God, and the heart never comes into spiritual commerce with the ports of heaven until God the Holy Ghost puts wind into the sails and speeds the ship into its haven. "Ye must be born again." If there be any real prayer in your heart, though you may not know the secret, God the Holy Ghost is there.

Now if He hears cries that do not come from Himself, how much more will He hear those that do! Perhaps you have been puzzling yourself to know whether your cry is a natural or a spiritual one. This may seem very important, and doubtless is so; but whether your cry be either the one or the other, still continue to seek the Lord. Possibly, you doubt whether natural cries are heard by God; let me assure you that they are. I remember saying something on this subject on one occasion in a certain Ultra-Calvinistic place of worship. At that time I was preaching to children, and was exhorting them to pray, and I happened to say that long before any actual conversion I had prayed for common mercies, and that God had heard my prayers. This did not suit my good brethren of the superfine school; and afterwards they all came round me professedly to know what I meant, but really to cavil and carp according to their nature and wont. "They compassed me about like bees; yea, like bees they compassed me about!" To say that God should hear the prayer of natural men was something worse than Arminianism, if indeed anything *could* be worse to them. "How could it be that God could hear a natural prayer?" And while I paused for a moment, an old woman in a red cloak pushed her way into the little circle round me, and said to them in a very forcible way, like a mother in Israel as she was, "Why do you raise this question; forgetting what God Himself has said! What is this you say, that God does not hear natural prayer? Why, does not he hear the young ravens when they cry unto Him, and do you think they offer spiritual prayers?" Straightway the men of war took to their heels; no defeat was more thorough; and for once in their lives they must have felt that they might possibly err.

Surely, brethren, this may encourage and comfort *you*. I am not going to set you just now to the task of finding out whether your prayers are natural or spiritual, whether they come from God's Spirit or whether they do not, because that might, perhaps, nonplus you; if the prayer proceeds from your very heart, we know how it got there though you may not. God hears the ravens, and I do believe He will hear you, and I believe, moreover, though I do not now want to raise the question in your heart, that He hears your prayer, because—though you may not know it— there is a secret work of the Spirit of God going on within you which is teaching you to pray.

VI. But I have mightier arguments, and nearer the mark. *When the young ravens cry they cry alone, but when you pray you have a mightier one than you praying with you.* Hear that sinner crying, "God be merciful to me a sinner." Hark! Do you hear that other cry which goes up with His? No, *you* do not hear it, because your ears are dull and heavy, but God hears it. There is another voice, far louder, and sweeter than the first, and far more prevalent, mounting up at the same moment and pleading, "Father, forgive them through my precious blood." The echo to the sinner's whisper is as majestic as the thunder's peal. Never sinner prays truly without Christ praying at the same time. You cannot see nor hear Him, but never does Jesus stir the depths of your soul by His Spirit without His soul being stirred too. Oh, sinner! your prayer when it comes before God is a very different thing from what it is when it issues forth from you.

Sometimes poor people come to us with petitions which they wish to send to some Company or great Personage. They bring the petition and ask us to have it presented for them. It is very badly spelt, very queerly written, and we can but just make out what they mean; but still there is enough to let us know what they want. First of all we make out a fair copy for them, and then, having stated their case, we put our own name at the bottom, and if we have any interest, of course they get what they desire through the power of the name signed at the foot of the petition. This is just what the Lord Jesus Christ does with our poor prayers. He makes a fair copy of them, stamps them with the seal of His own atoning blood, puts His own name at the foot, and thus they go up to God's throne. It is *your* prayer, but oh! it is *His* prayer too, and it is the fact of its being His prayer that makes it prevail. Now, this is a sledge-hammer argument: if the ravens prevail when they cry all alone, if their poor chattering brings them what they want of themselves, how much more shall the plaintive petitions of the poor trembling sinner prevail who can say, "For Jesus' sake," and who can clench all his own arguments with the blessed plea, "The Lord Jesus Christ deserves it; O Lord, give it to me for His sake."

I do trust that these seeking ones to whom I have been speaking, who have been crying so long and yet are afraid that they shall never be heard, may not have to wait much longer, but may soon have a gracious answer of peace; and if they shall not just yet get the desire of their hearts, I hope that they may be encouraged to persevere till the day of grace shall dawn. *You have a promise which the ravens have not,* and that might make another argument if time permitted us to dwell upon it. Trembler, having a promise to plead, never fear but that thou shalt speed at the throne of grace!

And now, let me say to the sinner in closing, IF YOU HAVE CRIED UNSUCCESSFULLY, STILL CRY ON. " Go again seven times," ay, and seventy times seven. Remember that the mercy of God in Christ Jesus is your only hope; cling to it, then, as a drowning man clings to the only rope within reach. If you perish praying for mercy through the precious blood, you will be the first that ever perished so. Cry on; just cry on; but oh! believe too; for believing brings the morning star and the daydawn. When John Ryland's wife Betty lay adying, she was in great distress of mind, though she had been for many years a Christian. Her husband said to her in his quaint but wise way, "Well, Betty, what ails you?" "Oh, John, I am dying, and I have no hope, John!" "But, my dear, where are you going then?" "I am going to hell!" was the answer. "Well," said he, covering up his deep anguish with his usual humour, and meaning to strike a blow that would be sure to hit the nail on the head and put her doubts to speedy flight, "what do you intend doing when you get there, Betty?" The good woman could give no answer, and Mr. Ryland continued, " Do you think you will pray when you get there?" "Oh, John," said she, "I should pray anywhere; I cannot help praying!" "Well, then," said he, "they will say, 'Here is Betty Ryland praying here; *turn her out ;* we won't have anybody praying here; *turn her out !'*" This strange way of putting it brought light to her

C

soul, and she saw at once the absurdity of the very suspicion of a soul really seeking Christ, and yet being cast away for ever from His presence. Cry on, soul; cry on! While the child can cry, it lives; and while you can besiege the throne of mercy, there is hope for you: but hear as well as cry, and believe what you hear, for it is by believing that peace is obtained.

What is it you are looking after? Some of you are expecting to see bright visions, but I hope you never may be gratified, for they are not worth a penny a thousand. All the visions in the world since the days of miracles, put together, are but mere dreams after all, and dreams are nothing but vanity. People eat too much supper and then dream; it is indigestion, or a morbid activity of brain, and that is all. If that is all the evidence you have of conversion you will do well to doubt it: I pray you never to rest satisfied with it; it is wretched rubbish to build your eternal hopes upon. Perhaps you are looking for very strange feelings —not quite an electric shock, but something very singular and peculiar. Believe me you need never feel the strange motions which you prize so highly. All those strange feelings which some people speak of in connection with conversion may or may not be of any good to them, but certain I am that they really have nothing to do with conversion so as to be at all necessary to it. I will put a question or two to you. Do you believe yourself to be a sinner? "Ay," say you. But supposing I put that word "sinner" away: do you mean that you believe you have broken God's law, that you are a good-for-nothing offender against God's government? Do you believe that you have in your heart, at any rate, broken all the commandments, and that you deserve punishment accordingly? "Yes," say you, "I not only believe that, but I feel it: it is a burden that I carry about with me daily." Now something more: do you believe that the Lord Jesus Christ can put all this sin of yours away? Yes, you do believe that. Then, can you trust Him to save you? you want saving; you cannot save yourself; can you trust *Him* to save you? "Yes," you say, "I already do that." Well, my dear friend, if you really trust Jesus, it is certain that you are saved, for you have the only evidence of salvation which is continual with any of us. There are other evidences which follow afterwards, such as holiness and the graces of the Spirit, but the only evidence that is continual with the best of men living is this—

> " Nothing in my hands I bring,
> Simply to thy cross I cling."

Can you use Jack the huckster's verse—

> " I'm a poor sinner and nothing at all,
> But Jesus Christ is my all-in-all"?

I HOPE you will go a great deal farther in experience on some points than this by and by, but I do not want you to advance an inch farther as to the ground of your evidence and the reason for your hope. Just stop there, and if now you look away from everything that is within you or without you to Jesus Christ, and trust to His sufferings on Calvary and to His whole atoning work as the ground of your acceptance before God, *you are saved*. You do not want anything more; you *have* passed from death unto life, "He that believeth on Him is not condemned." "He that believeth hath everlasting life." If I were to meet an angel presently in that aisle as I go out of my door into my vestry, and he should say—"Charles Spurgeon, I have come from heaven to tell you that you are pardoned," I should say to him—"I know *that* without your telling me anything of the kind; I know it on a great deal better authority than yours;" and if he asked me how I knew it, I should reply, "The word of God is better to me than the word of any angel, and *He* hath said it—'He that believeth on Him is not condemned'; I do believe on Him, and therefore I am not condemned, and I know it without an angel to tell me so."

Do not, you troubled ones, be looking after angels, and tokens, and evidences, and signs. If you rest on the finished work of Jesus you have already the best evidence of your salvation in the world; you have God's word for it; what more is needed? Cannot you take God's word? You can take your father's word; you can take your mother's word; why cannot you take God's word? Oh! what base hearts we must have to suspect God Himself! Perhaps you say you would not do such a thing. Oh! but you do doubt God, if you do not trust Christ; for "he that believeth not hath made God a liar." If you do not trust Christ, you do in effect say that God is a liar. You do not want to say that, do you?

Oh! believe the truthfulness of God! May the Spirit of God constrain you to believe the Father's mercy, the power of the Son's blood, the willingness of the Holy Ghost, to bring sinners to Himself! Come, my dear hearers, join with me in the prayer that you may be led by grace to see in Jesus all that you need.

" *Prayer* is a creature's strength, his very breath and being;
   Prayer is the golden key that can open the wicket of mercy;
   Prayer is the magic sound that saith to fate, so be it;
   Prayer is the slender nerve that moveth the muscles of Omnipotence.
   Wherefore, *pray*, O creature, for many and great are thy wants;
   Thy mind, thy conscience, and thy being, thy needs commend thee
      unto *prayer*,
   The cure of all cares, the grand panacea for all pains,
   Doubt's destroyer, ruin's remedy, the antidote to all anxieties."

ORDER AND ARGUMENT IN PRAYER

A Sermon

Text.—"Oh that I knew where I might find him! that I might come even to his seat! I would order my cause before him, and fill my mouth with arguments."—Job xxiii. 3, 4.

In Job's uttermost extremity he cried after the Lord. The longing desire of an afflicted child of God is once more to see His Father's face. His first prayer is not, "Oh that I might be healed of the disease which now festers in every part of my body!" nor even, "Oh that I might see my children restored from the jaws of the grave, and my property once more brought from the hand of the spoiler!" but the first and uppermost cry is, "Oh that I knew where I might find him—who is my God! that I might come even to His seat!" God's children run home when the storm comes on. It is the heaven-born instinct of a gracious soul to seek shelter from all ills beneath the wings of Jehovah. "He that hath made his refuge God," might serve as the title of a true believer. A hypocrite, when he feels that he has been afflicted by God, resents the infliction, and, like a slave, would run from the master who has scourged him; but not so the true heir of heaven, he kisses the hand which smote him, and seeks shelter from the rod in the bosom of that very God who frowned upon him.

You will observe that the desire to commune with God is intensified by the failure of all other sources of consolation. When Job first saw his friends at a distance, he may have entertained a hope that their kindly counsel and compassionate tenderness would blunt the edge of his grief; but they had not long spoken before he cried out in bitterness, "Miserable comforters are ye all." They put salt into his wounds, they heaped fuel upon the flame of his sorrow, they added the gall of their upbraidings to the wormwood of his griefs. In the sunshine of his smile they once had longed to sun themselves, and now they dare to cast shadows upon his reputation, most ungenerous and undeserved. Alas for a man when his wine-cup mocks him with vinegar, and his pillow pricks him with thorns! The patriarch turned away from his sorry friends and looked up to the celestial throne, just as a traveller turns from his empty skin bottle and betakes himself with all speed to the well. He bids farewell to earthborn hopes, and cries, "Oh, that I knew where I might find my God!"

My brethren, nothing teaches us so much the preciousness of the Creator as when we learn the emptiness of all besides. When you have been pierced through and through with the sentence, "Cursed is he that trusteth in man, and maketh flesh his arm," then will you suck unutterable sweetness from the divine assurance, "Blessed is he that trusteth in the Lord, and whose hope the Lord is." Turning away with bitter scorn from earth's hives, where you found no honey, but many sharp stings, you will rejoice in Him whose faithful word is sweeter than honey or the honeycomb.

It is further observable that though a good man hastens to God in his trouble, and runs with all the more speed because of the unkindness of his fellow men, yet sometimes the gracious soul is left without the comfortable presence of God. This is the worst of all griefs; the text is one of Job's deep groans, far deeper than any which came from him on account of the loss of his children and his property: "Oh that I knew where I might find HIM!" The worst of all losses is to lose the smile of my God. He now had a foretaste of the bitterness of his Redeemer's cry, "My God, my God, why hast thou forsaken me?" God's presence is always with His people in one sense, so far as secretly sustaining them is concerned, but His manifest presence they do not always enjoy. You may be beloved of God, and yet have no consciousness of that love in your soul. You may be as dear to His heart as Jesus Christ Himself, and yet for a small moment He may forsake you, and in a little wrath He may hide Himself from you.

But, dear friends, at such times the desire of the believing soul gathers yet greater intensity from the fact of God's light being withheld. The gracious soul addresseth itself with a double zeal to find out God, and sends up its groans, its entreaties, its sobs and sighs to heaven more frequently and fervently. "Oh that I knew where I might find Him!" Distance or labour are as nothing; if the soul only knew where to go she would soon overleap the distance. That seems to me to be the state of mind in which Job pronounced the words before us.

But we cannot stop upon this point, for the object of this morning's discourse beckons us onward. It appears that Job's end, in desiring the presence of God, was that he might pray to Him. He had prayed, but he wanted to pray as in God's presence. He desired to plead as before one whom he knew would hear and help him. He longed to state his own case before the seat of the impartial Judge, before the very face of the all-wise God; he would appeal from the lower courts, where his friends judged unrighteous judgment, to the Court of King's Bench—the High Court of heaven—there, saith he, "I would order my cause before Him, and fill my mouth with arguments."

In this latter verse Job teaches us how he meant to plead and intercede with God. He does, as it were, reveal the secrets o his closet, and unveils the art of prayer. We are here admitted into the guild of suppliants; we are shown the art and mystery of pleading; we have here taught to us the blessed handicraft and science of prayer, and if we can be bound apprentice to Job this morning, for the next hour, and can have a lesson from Job's Master, we may acquire no little skill in interceding with God.

There are two things here set forth as necessary in prayer— *ordering of our cause, and filling our mouth with arguments.* We shall speak of those two things, and then if we have rightly learned the lesson, a blessed result will follow.

I. First, IT IS NEEDFUL THAT OUR SUIT BE ORDERED BEFORE GOD.

There is a vulgar notion that prayer is a very easy thing, a kind of common business that may be done anyhow, without care or effort. Some thing that you have only to reach a book down and get through a certain number of very excellent words, and you have prayed and may put the book up again; others suppose that to use a book is superstitious, and that you ought rather to repeat extemporaneous sentences, sentences which come to your mind with a rush, like a herd of swine or a pack of hounds, and that when you have uttered them with some little attention to what you have said, you have prayed. Now neither of these modes of prayer were adopted by ancient saints. They appear to have thought a great deal more seriously of prayer than many do now-a-days.

The ancient saints were wont, with Job, to order their cause before God; that is to say, as a petitioner coming into Court does not come there without thought to state his case on the spur of the moment, but enters into the audience chamber with his suit well prepared, having moreover learned how he ought to behave himself in the presence of the great One to whom he is appealing. In times of peril and distress we may fly to God just as we are, as the dove enters the cleft of the rock, even though her plumes are ruffled; but in ordinary times we should not come with an unprepared spirit, even as a child comes not to his father in the morning till he has washed his face. See yonder priest; he has a sacrifice to offer, but he does not rush into the court of the priests and hack at the bullock with the first pole-axe upon which he can lay his hand, but when he rises he washes his feet at the brazen laver, he puts on his garments, and adorns himself with his priestly vestments; then he comes to the altar with his victim properly divided according to the law, and is careful to do according to the command, and he taketh the blood in a bowl and poureth it in an appropriate place at the foot of the altar, not throwing it just as may occur to him, and kindles the fire not with common flame, but with the sacred fire from off the altar, Now this ritual is all superseded, but the truth which it taught remains the same; our spiritual sacrifices should be offered with holy carefulness. God forbid that our prayer should be a mere leaping out of one's bed and kneeling down, and saying anything that comes first to hand; on the contrary, may we wait upon the Lord with holy fear and sacred awe. See how David prayed when God had blessed him—he went in before the Lord. Understand that; he did not stand outside at a distance, but he went in before the Lord and he sat down—for sitting is not a bad posture for prayer, let who will speak against it—and sitting down quietly and calmly before the Lord he then began to pray, but not until first he had thought over the divine goodness, and so attained to the spirit of prayer. Then by the assistance of the Holy Ghost did he open his mouth. Oh that we oftener sought the Lord is this style! Abraham may serve us as a pattern; he rose up early—here was his willingness; he went three days' journey—here was his zeal; he left his servants at the foot of the hill—here was his privacy; he carried the wood and the fire with him—here was his preparation; and lastly, he built the altar and laid the wood in order, and then took the knife—here was the devout carefulness of his worship. David puts it, "In the morning will I direct my prayer unto Thee, and will look up"; which I have frequently explained to you to mean that he marshalled his thoughts like men of war, or that he aimed his prayers like arrows. He did not take the arrow and put it on the bowstring and shoot, and shoot, and shoot anywhere; but after he had taken out the chosen shaft, and fitted it to the string, he took deliberate aim. He looked—looked well—at the white of the target; kept his eye fixed on it, directing his prayer, and then drew his bow with all his strength and let the arrow fly; and then, when the shaft had left his hand, what does he say? "I will look up." He looked up to see where the arrow went, to see what effect it had; for he expected an answer to his prayers, and was not as many who scarcely think of their prayers after they have uttered them. David knew that he had an engagement before him which required all his mental powers; he marshalled up his faculties and went about the work in a workmanlike manner, as one who believed in it and meant to succeed. We should plough carefully and pray carefully. The better the work the more attention it deserves. To be anxious in the shop and thoughtless in the closet is little less than blasphemy, for it is an insinuation that anything will do for God, but the world must have our best.

If any ask what order should be observed in prayer, I am not about to give you a scheme such as many have drawn out, in which adoration, confession, petition, intercession, and ascription are arranged in succession. I am not persuaded that any such order is of divine authority. It is to no mere mechanical order I have been referring, for our prayers will be equally acceptable, and possibly equally proper, in any form; for there are specimens of prayers, in all shapes, in the Old and New Testament. The true spiritual order of prayer seems to me to consist in something more than mere arrangement. It is most fitting for us first to feel that we are now doing something that is real; that we are about to address ourselves to God, Whom we cannot see, but Who is really present; Whom we can neither touch nor hear, nor by our senses can apprehend, but Who, nevertheless, is as truly with us as though we were speaking to a friend of flesh and blood like ourselves. Feeling the reality of God's presence, our mind will be led by divine grace into a humble state; we shall feel like Abraham, when he said, "I have taken upon myself to speak unto God, I that am but dust and ashes." Consequently we shall not deliver ourselves of our prayer as boys repeating their lessons, as a mere matter of rote, much less shall we speak as if we were rabbis instructing our pupils, or as I have heard some do, with the coarseness of a highwayman stopping a person on the road and demanding his purse of him; but we shall be humble yet bold petitioners, humbly importuning mercy through the Saviour's blood. When I feel that I am in the presence of God, and take my rightful position in that presence, the next thing I shall want to recognize will be that I have no right to what I am seeking, and cannot expect to obtain it except as a gift of grace, and I must recollect that God limits the channel through which He will give me mercy—He will give it to me through His dear Son. Let me put myself then under the patronage of the great Redeemer. Let me feel that now it is no longer I that speak but Christ that speaketh with me, and that while I plead, I plead His wounds, His life, His death, His blood, Himself. This is truly getting into order.

The next thing is to consider what I am to ask for? It is most proper in prayer, to aim at great distinctness of supplication. It is well not to beat round the bush in prayer, but to come directly to the point. I like that prayer of Abraham's, "Oh that Ishmael might live before thee!" There is the name and the person prayed for, and the blessing desired, all put in a few words, —"Ishmael might live before thee." Many persons would have used a roundabout expression of this kind, "Oh that our beloved offspring might be regarded with the favour which thou bearest

to those who," etc. Say "*Ishmael*," if you mean "Ishmael";
put it in plain words before the Lord.

Some people cannot even pray for the minister without using
such circular descriptives that you might think it were the parish
beadle, or somebody whom it did not do to mention too particularly. Why not be distinct, and say what we mean as well
as mean what we say? Ordering our cause would bring us to
greater distinctness of mind. It is not necessary, my dear brethren,
in the closet to ask for every supposable good thing; it is not
necessary to rehearse the catalogue of every want that you may
have, have had, can have, or shall have. Ask for what you
now need, and, as a rule, keep to present need; ask for your daily
bread—what you want now—ask for that. Ask for it plainly,
as before God, Who does not regard your fine expressions, and
to Whom your eloquence and oratory will be less than nothing
and vanity. Thou art before the Lord; let thy words be few, but
let thy heart be fervent.

You have not quite completed the ordering when you have
asked for what you want through Jesus Christ. There should be
a looking round the blessing which you desire, to see whether it is
assuredly a fitting thing to ask; for some prayers would never be
offered if men did but think. A little reflection would show to us
that some things which we desire were better let alone. We may,
moreover, have a motive at the bottom of our desire which is not
Christ-like, a selfish motive, which forgets God's glory and caters
only for our own ease and comfort. Now although we may ask
for things which are for our profit, yet still we must never let our
profit interfere in any way with the glory of God. There must be
mingled with acceptable prayer the holy salt of submission to
the divine will. I like Luther's saying, "Lord, I *will* have my
will of thee at this time." "What!" say you, "Like such an
expression as that?" I do, because of the next clause, which was,
"I will have my will, *for I know that my will is thy will.*" That is
well spoken, Luther; but without the last words it would have been
wicked presumption. When we are sure that what we ask for
is for God's glory, then, if we have power in prayer, we may say,
"I will not let Thee go except Thou bless me": we may come
to close dealings with God, and like Jacob with the angel we may
even put it to the wrestle and seek to give the angel the fall sooner
than be sent away without the benediction. But we must be
quite clear, before we come to such terms as those, that what we
are seeking is really for the Master's honour.

Put these three things together, the deep spirituality which
recognises prayer as being real conversation with the invisible
God—much distinctness which is the reality of prayer, asking

for what we know we want—and withal much fervency, believing the thing to be necessary, and therefore resolving to obtain it if it can be had by prayer, and above all these complete submission, leaving it still with the Master's will;—commingle all these, and you have a clear idea of what it is to order your cause before the Lord.

Still prayer itself is an art which only the Holy Ghost can teach us. He is the giver of all prayer. Pray for prayer—pray till you can pray; pray to be helped to pray, and give not up praying because thou canst not pray, for it is when thou thinkest thou canst not pray that thou art most praying; and sometimes when thou hast no sort of comfort in thy supplications, it is then that thy heart all broken and cast down is really wrestling, and truly prevailing with the Most High.

II. The second part of prayer is FILLING THE MOUTH WITH ARGUMENTS—not filling the mouth with words nor good phrases, nor pretty expressions, but filling the mouth with arguments. The ancient saints were wont to argue in prayer. When we come to the gate of mercy forcible arguments are the knocks of the rapper by which the gate is opened.

Why are arguments to be used at all? is the first enquiry; the reply being, Certainly not because God is slow to give, not because we can change the divine purpose, no because God needeth to be informed of any circumstance with regard to ourselves or of anything in connection with the mercy asked: the arguments to be used are for our own benefit not for his. He requires for us to plead with Him, and to bring forth our strong reasons, as Isaiah saith, because this will show that we feel the value of the mercy. When a man searches for arguments for a thing it is because he attaches importance to that which he is seeking. The best prayers I have ever heard in our prayer meetings have been those which have been fullest of argument. Sometimes my soul has been fairly melted down when I have listened to brethren who have come before God feeling the mercy to be really needed, and that they must have it, for they first pleaded with God to give it for this reason, and then for a second, and then for a third, and then for a fourth and a fifth, until they have awakened the fervency of the entire assembly.

My brethren, there is no need for prayer at all as far as God is concerned, but what a need there is for it on our own account! If we were not constrained to pray, I question whether we could even live as Christians. If God's mercies came to us unasked, they would not be half so useful as they now are, when they have to be sought for; for now we get a double blessing, a blessing in the obtaining, and a blessing in the seeking. The very act of prayer is a blessing. To pray is as it were to bathe one's-self in a cool purling stream, and so to escape from the heats of earth's summer sun. To pray is to mount on eagle's wings above the clouds and get into the clear heaven where God dwelleth. To pray is to enter the treasure-house of God and to enrich one's-self out of an inexhaustible storehouse. To pray is to grasp heaven in one's arms, to embrace the Deity within one's soul, and to feel one's body made a temple of the Holy Ghost. Apart from the answer prayer is in itself a benediction. To pray, my brethren, is to cast off your burdens, it is to tear away your rags, it is to shake off your diseases, it is to be filled with spiritual vigour, it is to reach the highest point of Christian health. God give us to be much in the holy art of arguing with God in prayer.

The most interesting part of our subject remains; it is a very rapid summary and catalogue of a few of the arguments which have been used with great success with God. It is well in prayer to plead with Jehovah *his attributes*. Abraham did so when he laid hold upon God's justice. Sodom was to be pleaded for, and Abraham begins, "Peradventure there be fifty righteous within the city: wilt thou also destroy and not spare the place for the fifty righteous that are therein? That be far from thee to do after this manner, to slay the righteous with the wicked: and that the righteous should be as the wicked, that be far from thee: Shall not the Judge of all the earth do right?" Here the wrestling begins. It was a powerful argument by which the patriarch grasped the Lord's left hand, and arrested it just when the thunder-bolt was about to fall. But there came a reply to it. It was intimated to him that this would not spare the city, and you notice how the good man, when sorely pressed, retreated by inches; and at last, when he could no longer lay hold upon justice, grasped God's right hand of mercy, and that gave him a wondrous hold when he asked that if there were but ten righteous there the city might be spared. So you and I may take hold at any time upon the justice, the mercy, the faithfulness, the wisdom, the long-suffering, the tenderness of God, and we shall find every attribute of the Most High to be, as it were, a great battering-ram, with which we may open the gates of heaven.

Another mighty piece of ordnance in the battle of prayer is *God's promise*. When Jacob was on the other side of the brook Jabbok, and his brother Esau was coming with armed men, he pleaded with God not to suffer Esau to destroy the mother and the children, and as a master reason he pleaded, "And thou saidst, Surely I will do thee good." Oh the force of that plea! He was holding God to His word: "Thou saidst." The attribute is a splendid horn of the altar to lay hold upon; but the promise, which has in it the attribute and something more, is a yet mightier holdfast. "Thou saidst." Remember how David put it. After Nathan had spoken the promise, David said at the close of his prayer, "Do as thou hast said." "Do as thou hast said." That is a legitimate argument with every honest man, and has *He* said, and shall He not do it? "Let God be true, and every man a liar." Shall not *He* be true? Shall *He* not keep His word? Shall not every word that cometh out of His lips stand fast and be fulfilled?

Solomon, at the opening of the temple, used this same mighty plea. He pleads with God to remember the word which He had spoken to His father David, and to bless that place. When a man gives a promissory note his honour is engaged. He signs his hand, and he must discharge it when the due time comes, or else he loses credit. It shall never be said that God dishonours His bills. The credit of the Most High never was impeached, and never shall be. He is punctual to the moment; He never is before His time, but He never is behind it. You shall search this Book through, and you shall compare it with the experience of God's people, and the two tally from the first to the last; and many a hoary patriarch has said with Joshua in his old age, "Not one good thing hath failed of all that the Lord God hath promised : all hath come to pass." My brother, if you have a divine promise, you need not plead that with an "if" in it; you may plead with a certainty. If for the mercy which you are now asking, you have God's solemnly pledged word, there will scarce be any room for the caution about submission to His will. You know His will : that will is in the promise; plead it. Do not give Him rest until He fulfil it. He meant to fulfil it, or else He would not have given it.

A third argument to be used is that employed by Moses, *the great name of God*. How mightily did he argue with God on one occasion upon this ground! "What wilt thou do for thy great name? The Egyptians will say, Because the Lord could not bring them into the land, therefore he slew them in the wilderness." There are some occasions when the name of God is very closely tied up with the history of His people. Sometimes in reliance upon a divine promise, a believer will be led to take a certain course of action. Now, if the Lord should not be as good as His promise, not only is the believer deceived, but the wicked world looking on would say, Aha! aha! Where is your God? Take the case of our respected brother, Mr. Müller, of Bristol. These many years he has declared that God hears prayer, and firm in that conviction, he has gone on to build house after house for the maintenance of orphans. Now, I can very well conceive that, if he were driven to a point of want of means for the maintenance of those thousand or two thousand children, he might very well use the plea, "What wilt thou do for thy great name?" And you, in some severe trouble, when you have fairly received the promise, may say, "Lord, Thou hast said, 'In six troubles I will be with thee, and in seven I will not forsake thee.' I have told my friends and neighbours that I put my trust in Thee, and if Thou do not deliver me now, where is Thy name? Arise, O God, and do this thing, lest Thy honour be cast into the dust."

So also may we plead *the sorrows of His people*. This is frequently done. Jeremiah is the great master of this art. He says, "Her Nazarites were purer than snow, they were whiter than milk, they were more ruddy in body then rubies, their polishing was of sapphire: their visage is blacker than a coal." "The precious sons of Zion, comparable to fine gold, how are they esteemed as earthen pitchers, the work of the hands of the potter!" He talks of all their griefs and straitnesses in the siege. He calls upon the Lord to look upon His suffering Zion; and ere long his plaintive cries are heard. Nothing so eloquent with the father as his child's cry; yes, there is one thing more mighty still, and that is a moan,—when the child is so sick that it is past crying, and lies moaning with that kind of moan which indicates extreme suffering and intense weakness. Who can resist that moan? Ah! and when God's Israel shall be brought very low so that they can scarcely cry but only their moans are heard, then comes the Lord's time of deliverance, and He is sure to show that He loveth His people. Dear friends, whenever you also are brought into the same condition you may plead your moanings, and when you see a church brought very low you may use her griefs as an argument why God should return and save the remnant of His people.

Brethren, it is good to plead with God *the past*. Ah, you experienced people of God, you know how to do this. Here is David's specimen of it: "Thou *hast* been my help. Leave me not, neither forsake me." He pleads God's mercy to him from his youth up. He speaks of being cast upon his God from his very birth, and then he pleads, "Now also, when I am old and grey-headed, O God, forsake me not." Moses also, speaking with God, says, "Thou *didst* bring this people up out of Egypt." As if he would say, "Do not leave Thy work unfinished; Thou hast begun to build, complete it. Thou hast fought the first battle; Lord, end the campaign! Go on till Thou gettest a complete victory." How often have we cried in our trouble, "Lord, Thou didst deliver me in such and such a sharp trial, when it seemed as if no help were near; Thou hast never forsaken me yet. I have set up my Ebenezer in Thy name. If Thou hadst intended to leave me why hast Thou showed me such things?

Hast Thou brought thy servant to this place to put him to shame?" Brethren, we have to deal with an unchanging God, who will do in the future what He has done in the past, because He never turns from His purpose, and cannot be thwarted in His design; the past thus becomes a very mighty means of winning blessings from Him.

There was once an occasion when the very Godhead of Jehovah made a triumphant plea for the prophet Elijah. On that august occasion, when he had bidden his adversaries see whether their god could answer them by fire, you can little guess the excitement there must have been that day in the prophet's mind. With what stern sarcasm did he say, "Cry aloud: for he is a god; either he is talking, or he is pursuing, or he is in a journey, or peradventure he sleepeth, and must be awakened." And as they cut themselves with knives, and leaped upon the altar, oh the scorn with which that man of God must have looked down upon their impotent exertions, and their earnest but useless cries! But think of how his heart must have palpitated, if it had not been for the strength of his faith, when he repaired the altar of God that was broken down, and laid the wood in order, and killed the bullock. Hear him cry, "Pour water on it. You shall not suspect me of concealing fire; pour water on the victim." When they had done so, he bids them "Do it a second time"; and they did it a second time; and then he says, "Do it a third time." And when it was all covered with water, soaked and saturated through, then he stands up and cries to God, "O God, let it be known that thou only art God." Here everything was put to the test. Jehovah's own existence was now put, as it were, at stake, before the eyes of men by this bold prophet. But how well the prophet was heard! Down came the fire and devoured not only the sacrifice, but even the wood, and the stones, and even the very water that was in the trenches, for Jehovah God had answered his servant's prayer. We sometimes may do the same, and say unto Him, "Oh, by thy Deity, by thine existence, if indeed thou be God, now show thyself for the help of thy people!"

Lastly, the grand Christian argument is *the sufferings, the death, the merit, the intercession of Christ Jesus.* Brethren, I am afraid we do not understand what it is that we have at our command when we are allowed to plead with God for Christ's sake. I met with this thought the other day: it was somewhat new to me, but I believe it ought not to have been. When we ask God to hear us, pleading Christ's name, we usually mean, "O Lord, thy dear Son deserves this of thee; do this unto me because of what he merits." But if we knew it we might go farther. Supposing you should say to me, you who keep a warehouse in the city, "Sir, call at my office, and use my name, and say that they are to give you such a thing." I should go in and use your name, and I should obtain my request as a matter of right and a matter of necessity.

This is virtually what Jesus Christ says to us. "If you need anything of God, all that the Father has belongs to me; go and use my name." Suppose you should give a man your cheque-book signed with your own name and left blank, to be filled up as he chose; that would be very nearly what Jesus has done in these words, "If ye ask anything in my name I will give it you." If I had a good name at the bottom of the cheque I should be sure that I should get it cashed when I went to the banker with it; so when you have got Christ's name, to whom the very justice of God hath become a debtor, and whose merits have claims with the Most High, when you have Christ's name there is no need to speak with fear and trembling and bated breath. Oh waver not and let not faith stagger! When thou pleadest the name of Christ thou pleadest that which shakes the gates of hell, and which the hosts of heaven obey, and God Himself feels the sacred power of that divine plea.

Brethren, you would do better if you sometimes thought more in your prayers of Christ's griefs and groans. Bring before the Lord His wounds, tell the Lord of His cries, make the groans of Jesus cry again from Gethsemane, and His blood speak again from that frozen Calvary. Speak out and tell the Lord that with such griefs, and cries, and groans to plead, thou canst not take a denial: such arguments as these will speed you.

III. If the Holy Ghost shall teach us how to order our cause, and how to fill our mouth with arguments, the result shall be that we SHALL HAVE OUR MOUTH FILLED WITH PRAISES. The man who has his mouth full of arguments in prayer shall soon have his mouth full of benedictions in answer to prayer. Dear friend, thou hast thy mouth full this morning, hast thou? what of? Full of complaining? Pray the Lord to rinse thy mouth out of that black stuff, for it will little avail thee, and it will be bitter in thy bowels one of these days. Oh have thy mouth full of prayer, full of it, full of arguments so that there is room for nothing else. Then come with this blessed mouthful, and you shall soon go away with whatsoever you have asked of God. Only delight thou thyself in Him, and He will give thee the desire of thy heart.

It is said—I know not how truly—that the explanation of the text, "Open thy mouth wide, and I will fill it," may be found in a very singular Oriental custom. It is said that not many years ago—I remember the circumstance being reported—the King of

Persia ordered the chief of his nobility, who had done something or other which greatly gratified him, to open his mouth, and when he had done so he began to put into his mouth pearls, diamonds, rubies, and emeralds, till he had filled it as full as it could hold, and then he bade him go his way. This is said to have been occasionally done in Oriental Courts towards great favourites. Now certainly whether that be an explanation of the text or not it is an illustration of it. God says, "Open thy mouth with arguments," and then He will fill it with mercies priceless, gems unspeakably valuable. Would not a man open his mouth wide when he had to have it filled in such a style? Surely the most simple-minded among you would be wise enough for that. Oh! let us then open wide our mouth when we have to plead with God. Our needs are great, let our askings be great, and the supply shall be great too. You are not straitened in Him; you are straitened in your own bowels. The Lord give you large-mouthedness in prayer, great potency, not in the use of language, but in employing arguments.

What I have been speaking to the Christian is applicable in great measure to the unconverted man. God give thee to see the force of it, and to fly in humble prayer to the Lord Jesus Christ and to find eternal life in Him.

PLEADING

A Sermon

Text.—"But I am poor and needy: make haste unto me, O God: thou art my help and my deliverer; O Lord, make no tarrying."—Psalm lxx. 5.

Young painters were anxious, in the olden times, to study under the great masters. They concluded that they should more easily attain to excellence if they entered the schools of eminent men. Men have paid large premiums that their sons may be apprenticed or articled to those who best understood their trades or professions; now, if any of us would learn the sacred art and mystery of prayer, it is well for us to study the productions of the greatest masters of that science. I am unable to point out one who understood it better than did the psalmist David. So well did he know how to praise, that his psalms have become the language of good men in all ages; and so well did he understand how to pray, that if we catch his spirit, and follow his mode of prayer, we shall have learned to plead with God after the most prevalent sort. Place before you, first of all, David's Son and David's Lord, that most mighty of all intercessors, and, next to him, you shall find David to be one of the most admirable models for your imitation.

We shall consider our text, then, as one of the productions of a great master in spiritual matters, and we will study it, praying all the while that God will help us to pray after the like fashion.

In our text we have the soul of a successful pleader under four aspects: we view, first, *the soul confessing*: "I am poor and needy." You have, next, *the soul pleading*, for he makes a plea out of his poor condition, and adds, "Make haste unto me, O God!" You see, thirdly, *a soul in its urgency*, for he cries, "Make haste," and he varies the expression but keeps the same idea: "Make no tarrying." And you have, in the fourth and last view, *a soul grasping God*, for the psalmist puts it thus: "Thou art my help and my deliverer"; thus with both hands he lays hold upon His God, so as not to let Him go till a blessing is obtained.

I. To begin with, then, we see in this model of supplication, A SOUL CONFESSING. The wrestler strips before he enters upon the contest, and confession does the like for the man who is about to plead with God. A racer on the plains of prayer cannot hope to win, unless, by confession, repentance, and faith, he lays aside every weight of sin.

D   45

Now, let it be ever remembered that confession is absolutely needful to the sinner when he first seeks a Saviour. It is not possible for thee, O seeker, to obtain peace for thy troubled heart, till thou shalt have acknowledged thy transgression and thine iniquity before the Lord. Thou mayest do what thou wilt, ay, even attempt to believe in Jesus, but thou shalt find that the faith of God's elect is not in thee, unless thou art willing to make a full confession of thy transgression, and lay bare thy heart before God. We do not usually think of giving charity to those who do not acknowledge that they need it: the physician does not send his medicine to those who are not sick. The blind man in the gospels had to feel his blindness, and to sit by the wayside begging; if he had entertained a doubt as to whether he were blind or not, the Lord would have passed him by. He opens the eyes of those who confess their blindness, but of others, He says, "Because ye say we see, therefore, your sin remaineth." He asks of those who are brought to Him, "What wilt thou that I should do unto thee?" in order that their need may be publicly avowed. It must be so with all of us: we must offer the confession, or we cannot gain the benediction.

Let me speak especially to you who desire to find peace with God, and salvation through the precious blood: you will do well to make your confession before God very frank, very sincere, very explicit. Surely you have nothing to hide, for there is nothing that you can hide. He knows your guilt already, but He would have *you* know it, and therefore He bids you confess it. Go into the details of your sin in your secret acknowledgments before God; strip yourself of all excuses, make no apologies; say, "Against thee, thee only, have I sinned, and done this evil in thy sight: that thou mightest be justified when thou speakest, and be clear when thou judgest." Acknowledge the evil of sin, ask God to make you feel it; do not treat it as a trifle, for it is none. To redeem the sinner from the effect of sin Christ Himself must needs die, and unless you be delivered from it you must die eternally. Therefore, play not with sin; do not confess it as though it were some venial fault, which would not have been noticed unless God had been too severe; but labour to see sin as God sees it, as an offence against all that is good, a rebellion against all that is kind; see it to be treason, to be ingratitude, to be a mean and base thing.

Never expect that the King of heaven will pardon a traitor, if he will not confess and forsake his treason. Even the tenderest father expects that the child should humble himself when he has offended, and he will not withdraw his frown from him till with tears he has said, "Father, I have sinned." Darest thou expect

God to humble Himself to thee, and would it not be so if He did not constrain thee to humble thyself to Him? Wouldst thou have Him connive at thy faults and wink at thy transgressions? He will have mercy, but He must be holy. He is ready to forgive, but not to tolerate sin; and, therefore, He cannot let thee be forgiven if thou huggest thy sins, or if thou presumest to say, "I have not sinned." Hasten, then, O seeker, hasten, I pray thee, to the mercy seat with this upon thy lips: "I am poor and needy, I am sinful, I am lost; have pity on me." With such an acknowledgment thou beginnest thy prayer well, and through Jesus thou shalt prosper in it.

Beloved hearers, the same principle applies to the church of God. We are praying for a display of the Holy Spirit's power in this church, and, in order to successful pleading in this matter, it is necessary that we should unanimously make the confession of our text, "I am poor and needy." We must own that we are powerless in this business. Salvation is of the Lord and we cannot save a single soul. The Spirit of God is treasured up in Christ, and we must seek Him of the great head of the church. We cannot command the Spirit, and yet we can do nothing without Him. He bloweth where he listeth. We must deeply feel and honestly acknowledge this. God will have His church before he blesses it know that the blessing is altogether from Himself. "Not by might nor be power, but by my Spirit, saith the Lord."

The career of Gideon was a very remarkable one, and it commenced with two most instructive signs. I think our heavenly Father would have all of us learn the very same lesson which he taught to Gideon, and when we have mastered that lesson, he will use us for his own purposes. You remember Gideon laid a fleece upon the barn floor, and in the morning all round was dry and the fleece alone was wet. God alone had saturated the fleece so that he could wring it out, and its moisture was not due to its being placed in a favourable situation, for all around was dry. He would have us learn that, if the dew of his grace fills any one of us with its heavenly moisture, it is not because we lie upon the barn-floor of a ministry which God usually blesses, or because we are in a church which the Lord graciously visits; but we must be made to see that the visitations of His Spirit are fruits of the Lord's sovereign grace, and gifts of His infinite love, and not of the will of man, neither by man. But then the miracle was reversed, for, as old Thomas Fuller says, "God's miracles will bear to be turned inside out and look as glorious one way as another."

The next night the fleece was dry and all around was wet. For sceptics might have said, "Yes, but a fleece would naturally attract moisture, and if there were any in the air, it would be likely to be absorbed by the wool." But, lo, on this occasion, the dew is not where it might be expected to be, even though it lies thickly all around. Damp is the stone and dry is the fleece. So God will have us know that He does not give us His grace because of any natural adaptation in us to receive it, and even where He has given a preparedness of heart to receive, He will have us understand that His grace and His Spirit are most free in action, and sovereign in operation: and that He is not bound to work after any rule of our making. If the fleece be wet He bedews it, and that not because it is a fleece, but because He chooses to do so. He will have all the glory of all His grace from first to last. Come then, my brethren, and become disciples to this truth. Consider that from the great Father of lights every good and perfect gift must come. We are His workmanship, he must work all our works in us. Grace is not to be commanded by our position or condition: the wind bloweth where it listeth, the Lord works and no man can hinder; but if He works not, the mightiest and the most zealous labour but in vain.

It is very significant that before Christ fed the thousands, He made the disciples sum up all their provisions. It was well to let them see how low the commissariat had become, for then when the crowds were fed they could not say the basket fed them, nor that the lad had done it. God will make us feel how little are our barley loaves, and how small our fishes, and compel us to enquire, "What are they among so many?" When the Saviour bade His disciples cast the net on the right side of the ship, and they dragged such a mighty shoal to land, He did not work the miracle till they had confessed that they had toiled all the night and had taken nothing. They were thus taught that the success of their fishery was dependent upon the Lord, and that it was not their nets, nor the way of dragging it, nor their skill and art in handling their vessels, but that altogether and entirely their success came from their Lord. We must get down to this, and the sooner we come to it the better.

Before the ancient Jews kept the passover, observe what they did. The unleavened bread is to be brought in, and the paschal lamb to be eaten; but there shall be no unleavened bread, and no paschal lamb, till they have purged out the old leaven. If you have any old strength and self-confidence; if you have anything that is your own, and is, therefore, leavened, it must be swept right out; there must be a bare cupboard before there can come in the heavenly provision, upon which the spiritual passover can be kept. I thank God when he cleans us out; I bless His name when He brings us to feel our soul poverty as a church, for then the blessing will be sure to come.

One other illustration will show this, perhaps, more distinctly still. Behold Elijah with the priests of Baal at Carmel. The test appointed to decide Israel's choice was this—the God that answereth by fire let him be God. Baal's priests invoked the heavenly flame in vain. Elijah is confident that it will come upon his sacrifice, but he is also sternly resolved that the false priests and the fickle people shall not imagine that he himself had produced the fire. He determines to make it clear that there is no human contrivance, trickery, or manoeuvre about the matter. The flame should be seen to be of the Lord, and of the Lord alone. Remember the stern prophet's command, "Fill four barrels with water, and pour it on the burnt sacrifice, and on the wood. And he said, Do it a second time; and they did it a second time. And he said, Do it a third time; and they did it a third time. And the water ran round about the altar; and he filled the trench also with water." There could be no latent fires there. If there had been any combustibles or chemicals calculated to produce fire after the manner of the cheats of the time, they would all have been damped and spoiled. When no one could imagine that man could burn the sacrifice, then the prophet lifted up his eyes to heaven, and began to plead, and down came the fire of the Lord, which consumed the burnt sacrifice and the wood, and the altar stones and the dust, and even licked up the water that was in the trench. Then when all the people saw it they fell on their faces, and they said, "Jehovah is the God; Jehovah is the God."

The Lord in this church, if He means greatly to bless us, may send us the trial of pouring on the water once, and twice, and thrice; He may discourage us, grieve us, and try us, and bring us low, till all shall see that it is not of the preacher, it is not of the organization, it is not of man, but altogether of God, the Alpha and the Omega, who workest all things according to the council of His will.

Thus I have shown you that for a successful season of prayer the best beginning is confession that we are poor and needy.

II. Secondly, after the soul has unburdened itself of all weights of merit and self-sufficiency, it proceeds to prayer, and we have before us A SOUL PLEADING. "I am poor and needy, make haste unto me, O God. Thou art my help and my deliverer: O Lord, make no tarrying." The careful reader will perceive four pleas in this single verse.

Upon this topic I would remark that it is the habit of faith, when she is praying, to use pleas. Mere prayer sayers, who do not pray at all, forget to argue with God; but those who would prevail bring forth their reasons and their strong arguments and they debate the question with the Lord. They who play at wrestling catch here and there at random, but those who are

really wrestling have a certain way of grasping the opponent—
a certain mode of throwing, and the like; they work according
to order and rule. Faith's art of wrestling is to plead with God,
and say with hold boldness, "Let it be thus and thus, for these
reasons." Hosea tells us of Jacob at Jabbok, "that there he spake
with us"; from which I understand that Jacob instructed us by
his example. Now, the two pleas which Jacob used were God's
precept and God's promise. First, he said, "Thou saidst unto me,
Return unto thy country and to thy kindred": as much as if he
put it thus:—"Lord, I am in difficulty, but I have come here
through obedience to thee. Thou didst tell me to do this; now,
since thou commandest me to come hither, into the very teeth
of my brother Esau, who comes to meet me like a lion, Lord,
Thou canst not be so unfaithful as to bring me into danger and
then leave me in it." This was sound reasoning, and it prevailed
with God. Then Jacob also urged a promise: "Thou saidst, I
will surely do thee good."

Among men, it is a masterly way of reasoning when you can
challenge your opponent with his own words: you may quote
other authorities, and he may say, "I deny their force"; but,
when you quote a man against himself, you foil him completely.
When you bring a man's promise to his mind, he must either
confess himself to be unfaithful and changeable, or, if he holds
to being the same, and being true to his word, you have him,
and you have won your will of him. Oh, brethren, let us learn
thus to plead the precepts, the promises, and whatever else may
serve our turn; but let us always have something to plead. Do
not reckon you have prayed unless you have pleaded, for pleading
is the very marrow of prayer. He who pleads well knows the
secret of prevailing with God, especially if he pleads the blood of
Jesus, for that unlocks the treasury of heaven. Many keys fit
many locks, but the master-key is the blood and the name of
Him that died but rose again, and ever lives in heaven to save
unto the uttermost. Faith's pleas are plentiful, and this is well,
for faith is placed in divers positions, and needs them all.

Faith will boldly plead all God's gracious relationships. She
will say to Him, "Art thou not the Creator? Wilt thou forsake
the work of thine own hands? Art thou not the Redeemer, thou
hast redeemed thy servant, wilt thou cast me away?" Faith
usually delights to lay hold upon the fatherhood of God. This is
generally one of her master points: when she brings this into the
field she wins the day. "Thou art a Father, and wouldst thou
chasten us though thou wouldst kill? A Father, and wilt thou not
provide? A Father, and hast thou no sympathy and no bowels
of compassion? A Father, and canst thou deny what thine own

child asks of thee?" Whenever I am impressed with the divine
majesty, and so, perhaps, a little dispirited in prayer, I find
the short and sweet remedy is to remember that, although He
is a great King, and infinitely glorious, I am His child, and no
matter who the father is, the child may always be bold with His
father, Yes, faith can plead any and all of the relationships in
which God stands to His chosen.

Faith, too, can ply heaven with the Divine Promises. If
you were to go to one of the banks in Lombard Street, and
see a man go in and out and lay a piece of paper on the tables
and take it up again and nothing more; if he did that several times
a day, I think there would soon be orders issued to the porter
to keep the man out, because he was merely wasting the clerk's
time, and doing nothing to purpose. Those city men who come
to the bank in earnest present their cheques, they wait till they
receive their money and then they go, but not without having
transacted real business. They do not put the paper down, speak
about the excellent signature and discuss the correctness of the
document, but they want their money for it, and they are not
content without it. These are the people who are always welcome
at the bank and not the triflers. Alas, a great many people play
at praying, it is nothing better. I say they play at praying, they
do not expect God to give them an answer, and thus they are
mere triflers, who mock the Lord. He who prays in a business-
like way, meaning what he says, honours the Lord. The Lord
does not play at promising, Jesus did not sport at confirming
the word by His blood, and we must not make a jest of prayer by
going about it in a listless unexpecting spirit.

The Holy Spirit is in earnest, and we must be in earnest also.
We must go for a blessing, and not be satisfied till we have it;
like the hunter, who is not satisfied because he has run so many
miles, but is never content till he takes his prey.

Faith, moreover, pleads the performances of God, she looks
back on the past and says, "Lord, thou didst deliver me on such
and such an occasion; wilt thou fail me now." She, moreover,
takes her life as a whole, and pleads thus: —

> " After so much mercy past,
>   Wilt thou let me sink at last?"

"Hast thou brought me so far that I may be put to shame at the
end?" She knows how to bring the ancient mercies of God,
and make them arguments for present favours. But your time
would all be gone if I tried to exhibit, even a thousandth part of
faith's pleas.

Sometimes, however, faith's pleas are very singular. As in this text, it is by no means according to the proud rule of human nature to plead—"I am poor and needy, make haste unto me, O God." It is like another prayer of David: "Have mercy upon mine iniquity, for it is great." It is not the manner of men to plead so, they say, "Lord, have mercy on me, for I am not so bad a sinner as some." But faith reads things in a truer light, and bases her pleas on truth. "Lord, because my sin is great, and thou art a great God, let thy great mercy be magnified in me."

You know the story of the Syrophenician woman; that is a grand instance of the ingenuity of faith's reasoning. She came to Christ about her daughter, and He answered her not a word. What do you think her heart said? Why, she said in herself, "It is well, for He has not denied me: since He has not spoken at all, He has not refused me." With this for an encouragement, she began to plead again. Presently Christ spoke to her sharply, and then her brave heart said, "I have gained words from Him at last, I shall have deeds from Him by-and-by." That also cheered her; and then, when He called her a dog. "Ah," she reasoned, "but a dog is a part of the family, it has some connection with the master of the house. Though it does not eat meat from the table, it gets the crumbs under it, and so I have thee now, great Master, dog as I am; the great mercy that I ask of Thee, great as it is to me, is only a crumb to Thee; grant it then I beseech Thee." Could she fail to have her request? Impossible! When faith hath a will, she always finds a way, and she will win the day when all things forebode defeat.

Faith's pleas are singular, but, let me add, faith's pleas are always sound; for after all, it is a very telling plea to urge that we are poor and needy. Is not that the main argument with mercy? Necessity is the very best plea with benevolence, either human or divine. Is not our need the best reason we can urge? If we would have a physician come quickly to a sick man, "Sir," we say, "it is no common case, he is on the point of death, come to him, come quickly!" If we wanted our city firemen to rush to a fire, we should not say to them, "Make haste, for it is only a small fire"; but, on the contrary, we urge that it is an old house, full of combustible materials, and there are rumours of petroleum and gunpowder on the premises; besides, it is near a timber yard, hosts of wooden cottages are close by, and before long we shall have half the city in a blaze." We put the case as bad as we can. Oh for wisdom to be equally wise in pleading with God, to find arguments everywhere, but especially to find them in our necessities.

They said two centuries ago that the trade of beggary was the easiest one to carry on, but it paid the worst. I am not sure about the last at this time, but certainly the trade of begging with God is a hard one, and undoubtedly it pays the best of anything in the world. It is very noteworthy that beggars with men have usually plenty of pleas on hand. When a man is hardly driven and starving, he can usually find a reason why he should ask aid of every likely person. Suppose it is a person to whom he is already under many obligations, then the poor creature argues, "I may safely ask of him again, for he knows me, and has been always very kind." If he never asked of the person before, then he says, "I have never worried him before; he cannot say he has already done all he can for me; I will make bold to begin with him." If it is one of his own kin, then he will say, "Surely you will help me in my distress, for you are a relation"; and if it be a stranger, he says, "I have often found strangers kinder than my own blood, help me, I entreat you." If he asks of the rich, he pleads that they will never miss what they give; and if he begs of the poor, he urges that they know what want means, and he is sure they will sympathise with him in his great distress. Oh that we were half as much on the alert to fill our mouths with arguments when we are before the Lord. How is it that we are not half awake, and do not seem to have any spiritual senses aroused. May God grant that we may learn the art of pleading with the eternal God, for in that shall rest our prevalence with Him, through the merit of Jesus Christ.

III. I must be brief on the next point. It is A SOUL URGENT: "Make haste unto me, O God. O Lord, make no tarrying." We may well be urgent with God, if as yet we are not saved, for our need is urgent; we are in constant peril, and the peril is of the most tremendous kind. O sinner, within an hour, within a minute, thou mayest be where hope can never visit thee; therefore, cry, "Make haste, O God, to deliver me: make haste to help me, O Lord!" Yours is not a case that can bear lingering: you have not time to procrastinate; therefore, be urgent, for your need is so. And, remember, if you really are under a sense of need, and the Spirit of God is at work with you, you will and must be urgent. An ordinary sinner may be content to wait, but a quickened sinner wants mercy now. A dead sinner will lie quiet, but a living sinner cannot rest till pardon is sealed home to his soul. If you are urgent this morning, I am glad of it, because your urgency, I trust, arises from the possession of spiritual life. When you cannot live longer without a Saviour, the Saviour will come to you, and you shall rejoice in Him.

Brethren, members of this church, the same truth holds good with you. God will come to bless you, and come speedily, when your sense of need becomes deep and urgent. Oh, how great is this church's need! We shall grow cold, unholy, and worldly; there will be no conversions, there will be no additions to our numbers; there will be diminuations, there will be divisions, there will be mischief of all kinds; Satan will rejoice, and Christ will be dishonoured, unless we obtain a larger measure of the Holy Spirit. Our need is urgent, and when we feel that need thoroughly, then we shall get the blessing which we want.

For my part, brethren and sisters, I desire to feel a spirit of urgency within my soul as I plead with God for the dew of His grace to descend upon this church. I am not bashful in this matter, for I have a license to pray. Mendicancy is forbidden in the streets, but, before the Lord I am a licensed beggar. Jesus has said, "men ought always to pray and not to faint." You land on the shores of a foreign country with the greatest confidence when you carry a passport with you, and God has issued passports to His children, by which they come boldly to His mercy seat; He has invited you, He has encouraged you, He has bidden you come to Him, and He has promised that whatsoever ye ask in prayer, believing, ye shall receive. Come, then, come urgently, come importunately, come with this plea, "I am poor and needy; make no tarrying, O my God," and a blessing shall surely come; it will not tarry. God grant we may see it, and give Him the glory of it.

IV. I am sorry to have been so brief where I had need to have enlarged, but I must close with the fourth point. Here is another part of the art and mystery of prayer—THE SOUL GRASPING GOD. She has pleaded, and she has been urgent, but now she comes to close quarters; she grasps the covenant angel with one hand, "Thou art my help," and with the other, "Thou art my deliverer." Oh, those blessed "my's," those potent "my's." The sweetness of the Bible lies in the possessive pronouns, and he who is taught to use them as the psalmist did, shall come off a conqueror with the eternal God.

Now sinner, I pray God thou mayest be helped to say this morning to the blessed Christ of God, "Thou art my help and my deliverer." Perhaps you mourn that you cannot get that length, but, poor soul, hast thou any other help? If thou hast, then thou canst not hold two helpers with the same hand. "Oh, no," say you, "I have no help anywhere. I have no hope except in Christ." Well, then, poor soul, since thy hand is empty, that empty hand was made on purpose to grasp thy Lord with: lay hold on Him! Say to Him, this day, "Lord, I will hang on thee as poor lame Jacob did; now I cannot help myself, I will cleave to Thee: I will not let Thee go except Thou bless me." "Ah, it would be too bold," says one. But the Lord loves holy boldness in poor sinners; He would have you be bolder than you think of being. It is an unhallowed bashfulness that dares not trust a crucified Saviour. He died on purpose to save such as thou art; let Him have His way with thee, and do thou trust Him.

"Oh," saith one, "but I am so unworthy." He came to seek and save the unworthy. He is not the Saviour of the self-righteous: he is the sinners' Saviour—"friend of sinners" is His name. Unworthy one, lay hold on him! "Oh," saith one, "but I have no right." Well, since you have no right, your need shall be your claim: it is all the claim you want. Methinks I hear one say, "It is too late for me to plead for grace." It cannot be: it is impossible. While you live and desire mercy, it is not too late to seek it. Notice the parable of the man who wanted three loaves. I will tell you what crossed my mind when I read it: the man went to his friend at midnight; it could not have been later; for if he had been a little later than midnight, it would have been early in the next morning, and so not late at all. It was midnight, and it could not be later; and so, if it is downright midnight with your soul, yet, be of good cheer, Jesus is an out of season Saviour; many of His servants are "born out of due time."

Any season is the right season to call upon the name of Jesus; therefore, only do not let the devil tempt thee with the thought that it can be too late. Go to Jesus now, go at once, and lay hold on the horns of the altar by a venturesome faith, and say, "Sacrifice for sinners, Thou art a sacrifice for me. Intercessor for the graceless, Thou art an intercessor for me. Thou Who distributest gifts to the rebellious, distribute gifts to me, for a rebel I have been. When we were yet without strength, in due time Christ died for the ungodly. Such am I, Master; let the power of Thy death be seen in me to save my soul."

Oh, you that are saved and, therefore, love Christ, I want you, dear brethren, as the saints of God, to practice this last part of my subject; and be sure to lay hold upon God in prayer. "Thou art my help and my deliverer." As a church we throw ourselves upon the strength of God, and we can do nothing without Him; but we do not mean to be without Him, we will hold Him fast. "Thou art my help and my deliverer." There was a boy at Athens, according to the old story, who used to boast that he ruled all Athens, and when they asked him how, he said, "Why, I rule my mother, my mother rules my father, and my father rules the city." He who knows how to be master of prayer will rule the heart of Christ, and Christ can and will do all things for His people, for the Father hath committed all things into His hands. You can be omnipotent if you know how to pray, omnipotent in all things which glorify God. What does the Word itself say? "Let him lay hold on my strength." Prayer moves the arm that moves the world. Oh for grace to grasp Almighty love in this fashion.

We want more holdfast prayer; more tugging, and gripping, and wrestling, that saith, "I will not let thee go." That picture of Jacob at Jabbok shall suffice for us to close with. The covenant angel is there, and Jacob wants a blessing from him: he seems to put him off, but no put-offs will do for Jacob. Then the angel endeavours to escape from him, and tugs and strives; so he may, but no efforts shall make Jacob relax his grasp. At last the angel falls from ordinary wrestling to wounding him in the very seat of his strength; and Jacob will let his thigh go, and all his limbs go, but he will not let the angel go. The poor man's strength shrivels under the withering touch, but in his weakness he is still strong: he throws his arms about the mysterious man, and holds him as in a death-grip. Then the other says, "Let me go, for the day breaketh." Mark, he did not shake him off, he only said, "Let me go"; the angel will do nothing to force him to relax his hold, he leaves that to his voluntary will. The valiant Jacob cries, "No, I am set on it, I am resolved to win an answer to my prayer. I will not let thee go except thou bless me." Now, when the church begins to pray, it may be at first, the Lord will make as though he would have gone further, and we may fear that no answer will be given. Hold on, dear breathren. Be ye steadfast, unmovable, notwithstanding all. By-and-by, it may be, there will come discouragements where we looked for a flowing success; we shall find brethren hindering, some will be slumbering, and others sinning; backsliders and impenitent souls will abound; but let us not be turned aside. Let us be all the more eager.

And if it should so happen that we ourselves become distressed and dispirited, and feel we never were so weak as we are now; never mind, brethren, still hold on, for when the sinew is shrunk the victory is near. Grasp with a tighter clutch than ever. Be this our resolution, "I will not let thee go except thou bless me." Remember the longer the blessing is coming the richer it will be when it arrives. That which is gained speedily by a single prayer is sometimes only a second rate blessing; but that which is gained after many a desperate tug, and many an awful struggle, is a full weighted and precious blessing. The children of importunity are always fair to look upon. The blessing which costs us the most prayer will be worth the most. Only let us be persevering in supplication, and we shall gain a broad far-reaching benediction for ourselves, the churches, and the world. I wish it were in my power to stir you all to fervent prayer; but I must leave it with the great author of all true supplication, namely, the Holy Spirit. May He work in us mightily, for Jesus' sake. Amen.

"THE THRONE OF GRACE"

A SERMON

Text.—"The throne of grace."—Hebrews iv. 16.

These words are found embedded in that gracious verse, "Let us therefore come boldly unto the throne of grace, that we may obtain mercy, and find grace to help in time of need"; they are a gem in a golden setting. True prayer is an approach of the soul by the Spirit of God to the throne of God. It is not the utterance of words, it is not alone the feeling of desires, but it is the advance of the desires to God, the spiritual approach of our nature towards the Lord our God. True prayer, is not a mere mental exercises nor a vocal performance, but it is deeper far than that—it in spiritual commerce with the Creator of heaven and earth. God is a Spirit unseen of mortal eye, and only to be perceived by the inner man; our spirit within us, begotten by the Holy Ghost at our regeneration, discerns the Great Spirit, communes with Him, prefers to Him its requests, and receives from Him answers of peace. It is a spiritual business from beginning to end; and its aim and object end not with man, but reach to God Himself.

In order to such prayer, the work of the Holy Ghost Himself is needed. If prayer were of the lips alone, we should only need breath in our nostrils to pray: if prayer were of the desires alone, many excellent desires are easily felt, even by natural men: but when it is the spiritual desire, and the spiritual fellowship of the human spirit with the Great Spirit, then the Holy Ghost Himself must be present all through it, to help infirmity, and give life and power, or else true prayer will never be presented, but the thing offered to God will wear the name and have the form, but the inner life of prayer will be far from it.

Moreover, it is clear from the connection of our text, that the interposition of the Lord Jesus Christ is essential to acceptable prayer. As prayer will not be truly prayer without the Spirit of God, so it will not be prevailing prayer without the Son of God. He, the Great High Priest, must go within the veil for us; nay, through His crucified person the veil must be entirely taken away; for, until then, we are shut out from the living God. The man who, despite the teaching of Scripture, tries to pray without a Saviour insults the Deity; and he who imagines that his own natural desires, coming up before God, unsprinkled with the precious blood, will be an acceptable sacrifice before God,

57

makes a mistake; he has not brought an offering that God can accept, any more than if he had struck off a dog's neck, or offered an unclean sacrifice. Wrought in us by the Spirit, presented for us by the Christ of God, prayer becomes power before the Most High, but not else.

In trying to speak of the text this morning, I shall take it thus: First, *here is a throne ;* then, secondly, *here is grace ;* then we will put the two together, and we shall see *grace on a throne ;* and putting them together in another order, we shall see *sovereignty manifesting itself, and resplendent in grace.*

I. Our text speaks of A THRONE—"The Throne of Grace." God is to be viewed in prayer as our Father; that is the aspect which is dearest to us; but still we are not to regard Him as though He were such as we are; for our Saviour has qualified the expression "Our Father," with the words "who art heaven"; and close at the heels of that condescending name, in order to remind us that our Father is still infinitely greater than ourselves, He has bidden us say, "Hallowed be thy name; thy kingdom come"; so that our Father is still to be regarded as a King, and in prayer we come, not only to our Father's feet, but we come also to the throne of the Great Monarch of the universe. The mercy-seat is a throne, and we must not forget this.

If prayer should always be regarded by us as an entrance into the courts of the royalty of heaven; if we are to behave ourselves as courtiers should in the presence of an illustrious majesty, then we are not at a loss to know the right spirit in which to pray. If in prayer we come to a throne, if is clear that our spirit should, in the first place, be one of *lowly reverence.* It is expected that the subject in approaching to the king should pay him homage and honour. The pride that will not own the king, the treason which rebels against the sovereign will should, if it be wise, avoid any near approach to the throne. Let pride bite the curb at a distance, let treason lurk in corners, for only lowly reverence may come before the King Himself when He sits clothed in His robes of majesty. In our case, the king before whom we come is the highest of all monarchs, the King of kings, the Lord of lords. Emperors are but the shadows of his imperial power. They call themselves kings by right divine, but what divine right have they? Common sense laughs their pretensions to scorn. The Lord alone hath divine right, and to Him only doth the kingdom belong. He is the blessed and only potentate. They are but nominal kings, to be set up and put down at the will of men, or the decree of providence, but He is Lord alone, the Prince of the kings of the earth.

" He sits on no precarious throne,
Nor borrows leave to be."

My heart, be sure that thou prostrate thyself in such a presence.
If He be so great, place thy mouth in the dust before Him, for
He is the most powerful of all kings; His throne hath sway in
all worlds; heaven obeys Him cheerfully, hell trembles at His
frown, and earth is constrained to yield Him homage willingly
or unwillingly. His power can make or can destroy. To create
or to crush, either is easy enough to Him. My soul, be thou sure
that when thou drawest nigh to the Omnipotent, Who is as a
consuming fire, thou put thy shoes from off thy feet, and worship
Him with lowliest humility.

Besides, He is the most Holy of all kings. His throne is a great
white throne, unspotted, and clear as crystal. "The heavens
are not pure in His sight, and He charged His angels with folly."
And thou, a sinful creature, with what lowliness shouldst thou
draw nigh to him. Familiarity there may be, but let it not be
unhallowed. Boldness there should be, but let it not be impertin-
ent. Still thou art on earth and He in heaven; still thou art a
worm of the dust, a creature crushed before the moth, and
He the Everlasting: before the mountains were brought forth,
He was God, and if all created things should pass away again,
yet still were He the same. My brethren, I am afraid we do not
bow as we should before the Eternal Majesty; but, henceforth,
let us ask the Spirit of God to put us in a right frame, that every
one of our prayers may be a reverential approach to the Infinite
Majesty above.

A throne, and therefore, in the second place, to be approached
with *devout joyfulness*. If I find myself favoured by divine grace to
stand amongst those favoured ones who frequent His courts,
shall I not feel glad? I might have been in His prison, but I
am before His throne: I might have been driven from His
presence for ever, but I am permitted to come near to Him,
even into His royal palace, into His secret chamber of gracious
audience, shall I not then be thankful? Shall not my thankfulness
ascend into joy, and shall I not feel that I am honoured, that I
am made the recipient of great favours when I am permitted
to pray? Wherefore is thy countenance sad, O suppliant, when
thou standest before the throne of grace? If thou wert before the
throne of justice to be condemned for thine iniquities, thy hands
might well be on thy loins; but now thou art favoured to come
before the King in His silken robes of love, let thy face shine with
sacred delight. If thy sorrows be heavy, tell them unto Him, for
He can assuage them; if thy sins be multiplied, confess them, for

He can forgive them. O ye courtiers in the halls of such a Monarch, be ye exceeding glad, and mingle praises with your prayers.

It is a throne, and therefore, in the third place, whenever it is approached, it should be with *complete submission*. We do not pray to God to instruct Him as to what He ought to do, neither for a moment must we presume to dictate the line of the divine procedure. We are permitted to say unto God, "Thus and thus would we have it,". but we must evermore add, "But, seeing that we are ignorant and may be mistaken—seeing that we are still in the flesh, and, therefore, may be actuated by carnal motives—not as we will, but as Thou wilt." Who shall dictate to the throne? No loyal child of God will for a moment imagine that he is to occupy the place of the King, but he bows before Him who has a right to be Lord of all; and though he utters his desire earnestly, vehemently, importunately, and pleads and pleads again, yet it is evermore with this needful reservation: "Thy will be done, my Lord; and, if I ask anything that is not in accordance therewith, my inmost will is that Thou wouldst be good enough to deny Thy servant; I will take it as a true answer. if Thou refuse me, if I ask that which seemeth not good in Thy sight." If we constantly remembered this, I think we should be less inclined to push certain suits before the throne, for we should feel, "I am here in seeking my own ease, my own comfort, my own advantage, and, peradventure, I may be asking for that which would dishonour God; therefore will I speak with the deepest submission to the divine decrees."

But, brethren, in the fourth place, if it be a throne, it ought to be approached with *enlarged expectations*. Well doth our hymn put it:

> " Thou art coming to a king:
> Large petitions with thee bring."

We do not come, as it were, in prayer, only to God's almonry where He dispenses His favours to the poor, nor do we come to the back-door of the house of mercy to receive the broken scraps, though that were more than we deserve; to eat the crumbs that fall from the Master's table is more than we could claim; but, when we pray, we are standing in the palace, on the glittering floor of the great King's own reception room, and thus we are placed upon a vantage ground. In prayer we stand where angels bow with veiled faces; there, even there, the cherubim and seraphim adore, before that selfsame throne to which our prayers ascend. And shall we come there with stunted requests, and narrow and contracted faith? Nay, it becomes not a King to be giving away pence and groats, He distributes pieces of broad gold; He scatters not as poor men must, scraps of bread and broken meat, but He makes a feast of fat things, of fat things full of marrow, of wines on the lees well refined.

When Alexander's soldier was told to ask what he would, he did not ask stintedly after the nature of his own merits, but he made such a heavy demand, that the royal treasurer refused to pay it, and put the case to Alexander, and Alexander in right kingly sort replied: "He knows how great Alexander is, and he has asked as from a king; let him have what he requests." Take heed of imagining that God's thoughts are as thy thoughts, and His ways as thy ways. Do not bring before God stinted petitions and narrow desires, and say, "Lord, do according to these," but, remember, as high as the heavens are above the earth, so high are His ways above your ways, and His thoughts above your thoughts, and ask, therefore, after a God-like sort, ask for great things, for you are before a great throne. Oh that we always felt this when we came before the throne of grace, for then He would do for us exceeding abundantly above what we ask or even think.

And, beloved, I may add, in the fifth place, that the right spirit in which to approach the throne of grace, is that of *unstaggering confidence*. Who shall doubt the King? Who dares impugn the Imperial word? It was well said that if integrity were banished from the hearts of all mankind besides, it ought still to dwell in the hearts of kings. Shame on a king if he can lie. The veriest beggar in the streets is dishonoured by a broken promise, but what shall we say of a king if his word cannot be depended upon? Oh, shame upon us, if we are unbelieving before the throne of the King of heaven and earth. With our God before us in all His glory, sitting on the throne of grace, will our hearts dare to say we mistrust Him? Shall we imagine either that He cannot, or will not, keep His promise? There, surely, is the place for the child to trust its Father, for the loyal subject to trust his monarch; and, therefore, far from it be all wavering or suspicion. Unstaggering faith should be predominant before the mercy-seat.

Only one other remark upon this point, and that is, that if prayer be a coming before the throne of God, it ought always to be conducted with the *deepest sincerity*, and in the spirit which makes everything *real*. If you are disloyal enough to despise the King, at least, for your own sake, do not mock Him to His face, and when He is upon His throne. If anywhere you dare repeat holy words without heart, let it not be in Jehovah's palace. If I am called upon to pray in public, I must not dare to use words that are intended to please the ears of my fellow-worshippers, but I must realise that I am speaking to God Himself, and that I

E

have business to transact with the great Lord. And, in my private prayer, if, when I rise from my bed in the morning, I bow my knee and repeat certain words, or when I retire to rest at night go through the same regular form, I rather sin than do anything that is good, unless my very soul doth speak unto the Most High. Dost thou think that the King of heaven is delighted to hear thee pronounce words with a frivolous tongue, and a thoughtless mind? Thou knowest Him not. He is a Spirit, and they that worship Him must worship Him in spirit and in truth.

Beloved, the gathering up of all our remarks is just this,— prayer is no trifle. It is an eminent and elevated act. It is a high and wondrous privilege. Under the old Persian Empire a few of the nobility were permitted at any time to come in unto the king, and this was thought to be the highest privilege possessed by mortals. You and I, the people of God, have a permit, a passport to come before the throne of heaven at any time we will, and we are encouraged to come there with great boldness; but still let us not forget that it is no mean thing to be a courtier in the courts of heaven and earth, to worship Him Who made us and sustains us in being. Truly, when we attempt to pray, we may hear the voice saying, out of the excellent glory, "Bow the knee." From all the spirits that behold the face of our Father who is in heaven, even now, I hear a voice which saith, "Oh, come let us worship and bow down, let us kneel before the Lord our Maker; for he is our God, and we are the people of his pasture and the sheep of his hand. O worship the Lord in the beauty of holiness; fear before him all the earth."

II. Lest the glow and brilliance of the word "throne" should be too much for mortal vision, our text now presents us with the soft, gentle radiance of that delightful word—"GRACE." We are called to the throne *of grace*, not to the throne of law. Rocky Sinai once was the throne of law, when God came to Paran with ten thousand of His holy ones. Who desired to draw near to that throne? Even Israel might not. Bounds were set about the mount, and if but a beast touched the mount, it was stoned or thrust through with a dart. O ye self-righteous ones who hope that you can obey the law, and think that you can be saved by it, look to the flames that Moses saw, and shrink, and tremble, and despair. To that throne we do not come now, for through Jesus the case is changed. To a conscience purged by the precious blood there is no anger upon the divine throne, though to our troubled minds—

> "Once 'twas a seat of burning wrath,
> And shot devouring flame;

> Our God appeared consuming fire,
> And *jealous* was his name."

And, blessed be God, we are not this morning to speak of the throne of ultimate justice. Before that we shall all come, and as many of us as have believed will find it to be a throne of grace as well as of justice; for, He who sits upon that throne shall pronounce no sentence of condemnation against the man who is justified by faith. It is a throne set up on purpose for the dispensation of grace; a throne from which every utterance is an utterance of grace; the sceptre that is stretched out from it is the silver sceptre of grace; the decrees proclaimed from it are purposes of grace; the gifts that are scattered adown its golden steps are gifts of grace; and He that sits upon the throne is grace itself. It is the throne of grace to which we approach when we pray; and let us for a moment or two think this over, by way of consolatory encouragement to those who are beginning to pray; indeed, to all of us who are praying men and women.

If in prayer I come before a throne of grace, then *the faults of my prayer will be overlooked*. In beginning to pray, dear friends, you feel as if you did not pray. The groanings of your spirit, when you rise from your knees are such that you think there is nothing in them. What a blotted, blurred, smeared prayer it is. Never mind; you are not come to the throne of Justice, else when God perceived the fault in the prayer He would spurn it,— your broken words, your gaspings, and stammerings are before a throne of grace. When any one of us has presented his best prayer before God, if he saw it as God sees it, there is no doubt He would make great lamentation over it; for there is enough sin in the best prayer that was ever prayed to secure its being cast away from God. But it is not a throne of justice I say again, and here is the hope for our lame, limping supplications. Our condescending King does not maintain a stately etiquette in His court like that which has been observed by princes among men, where a little mistake or a flaw would secure the petitioner's being dismissed with disgrace. Oh, no; the faulty cries of His children are not severely criticised by Him. The Lord High Chamberlain of the palace above, our Lord Jesus Christ, takes care to alter and amend every prayer before He presents it, and He makes the prayer perfect with His perfection, and prevalent with His own merits. God looks upon the prayer, as presented through Christ, and forgives all its own inherent faultiness. How this ought to encourage any of us who feel ourselves to be feeble, wandering, and unskilful in prayer. If you cannot plead with God as sometimes you did in years gone by, if you feel as if somehow or other you had grown rusty in the work of supplication, never give over, but come still, yea and come oftener, for it is not a throne of severe criticism, it is a throne of grace to which you come.

Then, further, inasmuch as it is a throne of grace, *the faults of the petitioner himself shall not prevent the success of his prayer.* Oh, what faults there are in us! To come before a throne how unfit we are—we, that are all defiled with sin within and without! Ah, I could not say to you, "Pray," not even to you saints, unless it were a throne of grace, much less could I talk of prayer to you sinners; but now I will say this to every sinner here, though he should think himself to be the worst sinner that ever lived, cry unto the Lord and seek Him while He may be found. A throne of grace is a place fitted for you: go to your knees; by simple faith go to your Saviour, for He, He it is Who is the throne of grace. It is in Him that God is able to dispense grace unto the most guilty of mankind. Blessed be God, neither the faults of the prayer nor yet of the suppliant shall shut out our petitions from the God Who delights in broken and contrite hearts.

If it be a throne of grace, then *the desires of the pleader will be interpreted.* If I cannot find words in which to utter my desires, God in His grace will read my desires without the words. He takes the meaning of His saints, the meaning of their groans. A throne that was not gracious would not trouble itself to make out our petitions; but God, the infinitely gracious One, will dive into the soul of our desires, and He will read there what we cannot speak with the tongue. Have you never seen the parent, when his child is trying to say something to him, and he knows very well what it is the little one has got to say, help him over the words and utter the syllables for him, and if the little one has half-forgotten what he would say, you have seen the father suggest the word: and so the ever-blessed Spirit, from the throne of grace, will help us and teach us words, nay, write in our hearts the desires themselves. We have in Scripture instances where God puts words into sinners' mouths. "Take with you words," saith he, "and say unto him, Receive us graciously and love us freely." He will put the desires, and put the expression of those desires into your spirit by His grace; He will direct your desires to the things which you ought to seek for; He will teach you your wants, though as yet you know them not; He will suggest to you His promises that you may be able to plead them; He will, in fact, be Alpha and Omega to your prayer, just as He is to your salvation; for as salvation is from first to last of grace, so the sinner's approach to the throne of grace is of grace from first to last. What comfort is this. Will we not, my dear friends, with the greater boldness draw near to this throne, as we suck out the sweet meaning of this precious word, "the throne of grace"?

If it be a throne of grace, then *all the wants of those who come to it will be supplied.* The King from off such a throne will not say, "Thou must bring to Me gifts, thou must offer to Me sacrifices." It is not a throne for receiving tribute; it is a throne for dispensing gifts. Come, then, ye who are poor as poverty itself; come ye that have no merits and are destitute of virtues, come ye that are reduced to a beggarly bankruptcy by Adam's fall and by your own trangressions; this is not the throne of majesty which supports itself by the taxation of its subjects, but a throne which glorifies itself by streaming forth like a fountain with floods of good things. Come ye, now, and receive the wine and milk which are freely given, yea, come buy wine and milk without money and without price. All the petitioner's wants shall be supplied, because it is a throne of grace.

"The throne of grace." The word grows as I turn it over in my mind, and to me it is a most delightful reflection that if I come to the throne of God in prayer, I may feel a thousand defects, but yet there is hope. I usually feel more dissatisfied with my prayers than with anything else I do. I do not believe that it is an easy thing to pray in public so as to conduct the devotions of a large congregation aright. We sometimes hear persons commended for preaching well, but if any shall be enabled to pray well, there will be an equal gift and a higher grace in it. But, brethren, suppose in our prayers there should be defects of knowledge: it is a throne of grace, and our Father knoweth that we have need of these things. Suppose there should be defects of faith: He sees our little faith and still doth not reject it, small as it is. He doth not in every case measure out his gifts by the degree of our faith, but by the sincerity and trueness of faith. And if there should be grave defects in our spirit even, and failures in the fervency or in the humility of the prayer, still, though these should not be there and are much to be deplored; grace overlooks all this, forgives all this, and still its merciful hand is stretched out to enrich us according to our needs. Surely this ought to induce many to pray who have not prayed, and should make us who have been long accustomed to use the consecrated art of prayer, to draw near with greater boldness than ever to the throne of grace.

III. But, now regarding our text as a whole, it conveys to us the idea of GRACE ENTHRONED. It is a throne, and who sits on it? It is grace personified that is here installed in dignity. And, truly, to-day grace is on a throne. In the gospel of Jesus Christ grace is the most predominant attribute of God. How comes it to be so exalted? We reply, well, grace has a throne *by conquest*. Grace came down to earth in the form of the Well-beloved, and it met with sin. Long and sharp was the struggle, and grace appeared to be trampled under foot of sin; but grace at last seized sin, threw it on its own shoulders, and, though all but crushed beneath the burden, grace carried sin up to the cross and nailed it there, slew it there, put it to death for ever, and triumphed gloriously. For this cause at this hour grace sits on a throne, because it has conquered human sin, has borne the penalty of human guilt, and overthrown all its enemies.

Grace, moreover, sits on the throne because it has established itself there *by right*. There is no injustice in the grace of God. God is as just when He forgives a believer as when He casts a sinner into hell. I believe in my own soul that there is as much and as pure a justice in the acceptance of a soul that believes in Christ as there will be in the rejection of those souls who die impenitent, and are banished from Jehovah's presence. The sacrifice of Christ has enabled God to be just, and yet the justifier of him that believeth. He who knows the word "substitution," and can spell its meaning aright, will see that there is nothing due to punitive justice from any believer, seeing that Jesus Christ has paid all the believer's debts, and now God would be unjust if He did not save those for whom Christ vicariously suffered, for whom His righteousness was provided, and to whom it is imputed. Grace is on the throne by conquest, and sits there by right.

Grace is enthroned this day, brethren, because Christ has finished His work and gone into the heavens. It is enthroned *in power*. When we speak of its throne, we mean that it has unlimited might. Grace sits not on the footstool of God; grace stands not in the courts of God, but it sits on the throne; it is the regnant attribute; it is the king to-day. This is the dispensation of grace, the year of grace: grace reigns through righteousness unto eternal life. We live in the era of reigning grace, for seeing He ever liveth to make intercession for the sons of men, Jesus is able also to save them to the uttermost that come unto God by Him. Sinner, if you were to meet grace in the by-way, like a traveller on his journey, I would bid you make its acquaintance and ask its influence; if you should meet grace as a merchant on the exchange, with treasure in his hand, I would bid you court its friendship, it will enrich you in the hour of poverty; if you should see grace as one of the peers of heaven, highly exalted, I would bid you seek to get its ear; but, oh, when grace sits on the throne, I beseech you close in with it at once. It can be no higher, it can be no greater, for it is written "God is love," which is an *alias* for grace. Oh, come and bow before it; come and adore the infinite mercy and grace of God. Doubt not, halt not, hesitate not. Grace is reigning; grace is God; God is love. There is a rainbow round about the throne like unto an emerald, the emerald of his compassion and his love. O happy souls that can believe this, and believing it can come at once and glorify grace by becoming instances of its power.

IV. Lastly, our text, if rightly read, has in it SOVEREIGNTY RESPLENDENT IN GLORY,—THE GLORY OF GRACE. The mercy seat is a throne; though grace is there, it is still a throne. Grace does not displace sovereignty. Now, the attribute of sovereignty is very high and terrible; its light is like unto a jasper stone, most precious, and like unto a sapphire stone, or, as Ezekiel calls it, "the terrible crystal." Thus saith the King, the Lord of hosts, "I will have mercy on whom I will have mercy, and I will have compassion on whom I will have compassion." "Who art thou, O man, that repliest against God? Shall the thing formed say to him that formed it, Why hast thou made me thus?" "Hath not the potter power over the clay to make of the same lump one vessel unto honour and another unto dishonour?" But, ah! lest any of you should be downcast by the thought of His sovereignty, I invite you to the text. It is a throne,—there is sovereignty; but to every soul that knows how to pray, to every soul that by faith comes to Jesus, the true mercy seat, divine sovereignty wears no dark and terrible aspect, but is full of love. It is a throne of grace; from which I gather that the sovereignty of God to a believer, from which I pleader, to one who comes to God in Christ, is always exercised in pure grace. To you, to you who come to God in prayer, the sovereignty always runs thus: "I will have mercy on that sinner; though he deserves it not, though in him there is no merit, yet because I can do as I will with my own, I will bless him, I will make him my child, I will accept him; he shall be mine in the day when I make up my jewels."

There are these two or three things to be thought of, and I have done. On the throne of grace sovereignty has placed itself under bonds of love. God will do as He wills; but, on the mercy-seat, He is under bonds—bonds of His own making, for He has entered into covenant with Christ, and so into covenant with His chosen. Though God is and ever must be a sovereign, He never will break His covenant, nor alter the word that is gone out of His mouth. He cannot be false to a covenant of His own making. When I come to God in Christ, to God on the mercy-seat, I need not imagine that by any act of sovereignty God will set aside His covenant. That cannot be: it is impossible.

Moreover, on the throne of grace, God is again bound to us by His promises. The covenant contains in it many gracious promises, exceeding great and precious. "Ask and it shall be given you; seek and ye shall find; knock and it shall be opened unto you." Until God had said that word or a word to that effect, it was at His own option to hear prayer or not, but it is not so now; for now, if it be true prayer offered through Jesus Christ, His truth binds Him to hear it. A man may be perfectly free, but the moment he makes a promise, he is not free to break it; and the everlasting God wants not to break His promise. He delights to fulfil it. He hath declared that all His promises are yea and amen in Christ Jesus; but, for our consolation when we survey God under the high and terrible aspect of a sovereign, we have this to reflect on, that He is under covenant bonds of promise to be faithful to the souls that seek him. His throne must be a throne of grace to His people.

And, once more, and sweetest thought of all, every covenant promise has been endorsed and sealed with blood, and far be it from the everlasting God to pour scorn upon the blood of His dear Son. When a king has given a charter to a city, he may before have been absolute, and there may have been nothing to check his prerogatives, but when the city has its charter, then it pleads its rights before the king. Even thus God has given to His people a charter of untold blessings, bestowing upon them the sure mercies of David. Very much of the validity of a charter depends upon the signature and the seal, and, my brethren, how sure is the charter of covenant grace. The signature is the hand-writing of God Himself, and the seal is the blood of the Only-begotten. The covenant is ratified with blood, the blood of His own dear Son. It is not possible that we can plead in vain with God when we plead the blood-sealed covenant, ordered in all things and sure. Heaven and earth shall pass away, but the power of the blood of Jesus with God can never fail. It speaks when we are silent, and it prevails when we are defeated. Better things than that of Abel doth it ask for, and its cry is heard. Let us come boldly, for we bear the promise in our hearts. When we feel alarmed because of the sovereignty of God, let us cheerfully sing—

> " The gospel bears my spirit up,
>   A faithful and unchanging God
> Lays the foundation for my hope
>   In oaths, and promises, and blood."

May God the Holy Spirit help us to use aright from this time forward "the throne of grace." Amen.

PRAYER CERTIFIED OF SUCCESS

A Sermon

Text.—"And I say unto you, Ask, and it shall be given you; seek, and ye shall find; knock, and it shall be opened unto you. For every one that asketh receiveth; and he that seeketh findeth; and to him that knocketh it shall be opened."—Luke xi. 9–10.

To seek aid in time of distress from a supernatural being is an instinct of human nature. We say not that human nature unrenewed ever offers truly spiritual prayer, or ever exercises saving faith in the living God; but still, like a child crying in the dark, with painful longing for help from somewhere or other, it scarce knows where, the soul in deep sorrow almost invariably cries to some supernatural being for succour. None have been more ready to pray in time of trouble than those who have ridiculed prayer in their prosperity; and probably no prayers have been more true to the feelings of the hour than those which atheists have offered under the pressure of the fear of death.

In one of his papers in the *Tattler*, Addison describes a man, who, on board ship, loudly boasted of his atheism. A brisk gale springing up, he fell upon his knees and confessed to the chaplain that he had been an atheist. The common seamen who had never heard the word before, thought it had been some strange fish, but were more surprised when they saw it was a man, and learned out of his own mouth "that he never believed till that day that there was a God." One of the old tars whispered to the boatswain that it would be a good deed to heave him overboard, but this was a cruel suggestion, for the poor creature was already in misery enough—his atheism had evaporated, and he in mortal terror cried to God to have mercy upon him.

Similar incidents have occurred, not once nor twice. Indeed, so frequently does boastful scepticism come down with a run at the last that we always expect it to do so. Take away unnatural restraint from the mind, and it may be said of all men that, like the comrades of Jonah, they cry every man unto his God in their trouble. As birds to their nests, and hinds to their coverts, so men in agony fly to a superior being for succour in the hour of need.

By instinct man turned to his God in Paradise; and now, though He is to a sad degree a discrowned monarch, there lingers in His memory shadows of what He was, and remembrances of where His strength must still be found. Therefore, no matter where you

find a man, you meet one who in his distress will ask for supernatural help. I believe in the truthfulness of this instinct, and that
man prays because there is something in prayer. As when the
Creator gives His creature the power of thirst, it is because water
exists to meet its thirst; and as when He creates hunger there is
food to correspond to the appetite; so when He inclines men to
pray it is because prayer has a corresponding blessing connected
with it.

We find a powerful reason for expecting prayer to be effectual
in the fact that it is an institution of God. In God's word we
are over and over again commanded to pray. God's institutions
are not folly. Can I believe that the infinitely wise God has
ordained for me an exercise which is ineffectual, and is no more
than child's play? Does He bid me pray, and yet has prayer
no more result than if I whistled to the wind, or sang to a grove
of trees? If there be no answer to prayer, prayer is a monstrous
absurdity and God is the author of it; which it is blasphemy to
assert. No man who is not a fool will continue to pray when you
have once proved to him that prayer has no effect with God,
and never receives an answer. Prayer is a work for idiots and
madmen, and not for sane persons, if it be, indeed, true, that its
effects end with the man who prays!

I shall not this morning enter into any arguments upon the
matter; rather, I am coming to my text, which to me, at least,
and to you who are followers of Christ, is the end of all controversy.
Our Saviour knew right well that many difficulties would arise
in connection with prayer which might tend to stagger His
disciples, and therefore He has balanced every opposition by an
overwhelming assurance. Read those words, "*I say unto you*,"
I—your Teacher, your Master, your Lord, your Saviour, your
God: "I say unto you, Ask, and it shall be given you; seek,
and ye shall find; knock, and it shall be opened unto you."

In the text our Lord meets all difficulties first by *giving us the
weight of His own authority*, "I say unto you"; next by *presenting
us with a promise*, "Ask, and it shall be given you," and so on;
and then by *reminding us of an indisputable fact*, "everyone that asketh
receiveth." Here are three mortal wounds for a Christian's
doubts as to prayer.

I. First, then, OUR SAVIOUR GIVES TO US THE WEIGHT OF HIS
OWN AUTHORITY, "*I say unto you.*" The first mark of a follower
of Christ is, that he believes his Lord. We do not follow the
Lord at all if we raise any questions upon points whereupon He
speaks positively. Though a doctrine should be surrounded with
ten thousand difficulties, the *ipse dixit* of the Lord Jesus sweeps
them all away, so far as true Christians are concerned. Our

Master's declaration is all the argument we want, "I say unto you," is our logic. Reason! we see thee at thy best in Jesus, for He is made of God unto us wisdom. He cannot err, He cannot lie, and if He saith, "I say unto you," there is an end of all debate.

But, brethren, there are certain reasons which should lead us the more confidently to rest in our Master's word upon this point. There is power in every word of the Lord Jesus, but there is special force in the utterance before us. It has been objected to prayer that it is not possible that it should be answered, because the laws of nature are unalterable, and they must and will go on whether men pray or not. To us it does not seem needful to prove that the laws of nature are disturbed. God can work miracles, and He may work them yet again as He has done in days of yore, but it is no part of the Christian faith that God must needs work miracles in order to answer the prayers of His servants. When a man in order to fulfil a promise has to dis-arrange all his affairs, and, so to speak, to stop all his machinery, it proves that he is but a man, and that his wisdom and power are limited; but He is God indeed, who without reversing the engine, or removing a single cog from a wheel, fulfils the desires of His people as they come up before Him. The Lord is so omnipotent that He can work results tantamount to miracles without in the slightest degree suspending any one of His laws. He did, as it were, in the olden times, stop the machinery of the universe to answer prayer, but now, with equally godlike glory, He orders events so as to answer believing prayers, and yet suspends no natural law.

But this is far from being our only or our main comfort; that lies in the fact that we hear the voice of one who is competent to speak upon the matter, and He says, "I say unto you, Ask and it shall be given you." Whether the laws of nature are reversible or irreversible, "Ask and it shall be given you; seek and ye shall find." Now, Who is He that speaketh thus? It is He that made all things, without Whom was not anything made that was made. Cannot He speak to this point. O thou eternal Word, thou who wast in the beginning with God, balancing the clouds and fastening the foundations of the earth, thou knowest what the laws and the unalterable constitutions of nature may be, and if thou sayest, "Ask and it shall be given you," then assuredly it will be so, be the laws of nature what they may. Besides, our Lord is by us adored as the sustainer of all things; and, seeing that all the laws of nature are only operative through His power, and are sustained in their motion by His might, He must be cognizant of the motion of all the forces in the world; and if

He says, "Ask and it shall be given you," He does not speak in ignorance, but knows what He affirms. We may be assured that there are no forces which can prevent the fulfilment of the Lord's own word. From the Creator and the Sustainer, the word "I say unto you," settles all controversy for ever.

But another objection has been raised which is very ancient indeed, and has a great appearance of force. It is raised not so much by sceptics, as by those who hold a part of the truth; it is this—that prayer can certainly produce no results, because the decrees of God have settled everything, and those decrees are immutable. Now we have no desire to deny the assertion that the decrees of God have settled all events. It is our full belief that God has foreknown and predestinated everything that happeneth in heaven above or in the earth beneath, and that the foreknown station of a reed by the river is as fixed as the station of a king, and "the chaff from the hand of the winnower is steered as the stars in their courses." Predestination embraceth the great and the little, and reacheth unto all things; the question is, wherefore pray? Might it not as logically be asked wherefore breathe, eat, move, or do anything? We have an answer which satisfies us, namely, that our prayers are in the predestination, and that God has as much ordained His people's prayers as anything else, and when we pray we are producing links in the chain of ordained facts. Destiny decrees that I should pray— I pray; destiny decrees that I shall be answered, and the answer comes to me.

But we have a better answer than all this. Our Lord Jesus Christ comes forward, and He says to us this morning, " My dear children, the decrees of God need not trouble you, there is nothing in them inconsistent with your prayers being heard. 'I say unto you, Ask, and it shall be given you.'" Now, who is He that says this? Why it is He that has been with the Father from the beginning—"the same was in the beginning with God"— and He knows what the purposes of the Father are and what the heart of God is, for He has told us in another place, "the Father himself loveth you." Now since He knows the decrees of the Father, and the heart of the Father, He can tell us with the absolute certainty of an eye-witness that there is nothing in the eternal purposes in conflict with this truth, that he that asketh receiveth, and he that seeketh findeth. He has read the decrees from beginning to end: hath He not taken the book, and loosed the seven seals thereof, and declared the ordinances of heaven? He tells you there is nothing there inconsistent with your bended knee and streaming eye, and with the Father's opening the windows of heaven to shower upon you the blessings which you seek. Moreover, He is Himself God: the purposes of heaven are His own purposes, and He who ordained the purpose here gives the assurance that there is nothing in it to prevent the efficacy of prayer. "I say unto you." O ye that believe in Him, your doubts are scattered to the winds, ye know that He heareth prayer.

But sometimes there arises in our mind a third difficulty, which is associated with our own judgment of ourselves and our estimate of God. We feel that God is very great, and we tremble in the presence of His majesty, we feel that we are very little, and that, in addition, we are also vile; and it does seem a thing incredible that such guilty nothings should have power to move the arm which moves the world. I wonder not if that fear should often hamper us in prayer. But Jesus answers it so sweetly: He says— "I say unto you, Ask and it shall be given you." And I ask again, who is it that says, "I say unto you"? Why, it is He who knows both the greatness of God and the weakness of man. He is God, and out of the excellent Majesty I think I hear Him say, "I say unto you, Ask, and it shall be given you." But He is also man like ourselves, and He says, "Dread not your littleness, for I, bone of your bone, and flesh of your flesh, assure you that God heareth man's prayer."

And yet, again, if the dread of sin should haunt us, and our own sorrow should depress us, I would remind you that Jesus Christ, when He says, "I say unto you," gives us the authority, not only of His person, but of His experience. Jesus was wont to pray. Never any prayed as He did. Nights were spent in prayer by Him, and whole days in earnest intercession; and He says to us, "I say unto you, Ask, and it shall be given you." I think I see Him coming fresh from the heather of the hills, among which He had knelt all night to pray, and He says, "My disciples, Ask, and it shall be given you, for I have prayed, and it has been given unto me." He was heard in that He feared, and therefore He saith to us, "I say unto you, knock and it shall be opened unto you." Ay, and I think I hear Him speak thus from the cross, with His face bright with the first beam of sunlight after He had borne our sins in His own body on the tree, and had suffered all our griefs to the last pang. He had cried, "My God, my God, why hast thou forsaken me," and now, having received an answer, He cries in triumph, "It is finished," and, in so doing, bids us also "ask, and it shall be given us." Jesus has proved the power of prayer.

Remember, too, that if Jesus our Lord could speak so positively here, there is a yet greater reason for believing Him now, for He has gone within the veil, He sits at the right hand of God, even the Father, and the voice does not come to us from the man of poverty, wearing a garment without seam, but from the enthroned priest with the golden girdle about His loins, for it is He who now saith, from the right hand of God: "I say unto you, Ask, and it shall be given you." Do you not believe in His name? How then can a prayer that is sincerely offered in that name fall to the ground? When you present your petition in Jesu's name, a part of His authority clothes your prayers. If your prayer be rejected, Christ is dishonoured: you cannot believe that. You have trusted him, then believe that prayer offered through Him must and shall win the day.

We cannot tarry longer on this point, but we trust the Holy Spirit will impress it upon all our hearts.

II. We will now remember that OUR LORD PRESENTS US WITH A PROMISE.

Note that the promise is given to several varieties of prayer. "I say unto you, Ask, and it shall be given you; seek, and ye shall find; knock and it shall be opened unto you." The text clearly asserts that all forms of true prayer shall be heard, provided they be presented through Jesus Christ, and are for promised blessings. Some are vocal prayers, men *ask ;* never should we fail to offer up every day and continually the prayer which is uttered by the tongue, for the promise is that the asker shall be heard. But there are others who, not neglecting vocal prayer, are far more abundant in active prayer, for by humble and diligent use of the means they *seek* for the blessings which they need. Their heart speaks to God by its longings, strivings, emotions, and labours. Let them not cease seeking, for they shall surely find. There are others who, in their earnestness, combine the most eager forms, both acting and speaking, for *knocking* is a loud kind of asking, and a vehement form of seeking. So the prayers grow from asking—which is the statement, to seeking—which is the pleading; and to knocking—which is the importuning; to each of these stages of prayer there is a distinct promise. He that asks shall have, what did he ask for more? but he that seeks going further shall find, shall enjoy, shall grasp, shall know that he has obtained; and he who knocks shall go further still, for he shall understand, and to him shall the precious thing be opened—he shall not merely have the blessing and enjoy it, but he shall comprehend it, shall "understand with all saints, what are the heights and depths."

I want, however, you to notice this fact, which covers all—whatever form your prayer may assume it shall succeed. If you only ask you shall receive, if you seek you shall find, if you knock it shall be opened, but in each case according to your faith shall it be unto you. The clauses of the promise before us are not put as we say in law, jointly: he that asks and seeks and knocks shall receive, but they are put severally—he that asks shall have, he that seeks shall find, he that knocks shall have it opened. It is not when we combine the whole three that we get the blessing, though doubtless if we did combine them, we should get the combined reply; but if we exercise only one of these three forms of prayer, we shall still get that which our souls seek after.

These three methods of prayer exercise a variety of our graces. It is a gloss of the fathers upon this passage that faith asks, hope seeks, and love knocks, and the gloss is worth repeating. Faith asks because she believes God will give; hope having asked expects, and therefore seeks for the blessing; love comes nearer still, and will not take a denial from God, but desireth to enter into His house, and to sup with Him, and, therefore, knocks at His door till He opens. But, again, let us come back to the old point; it matters not which grace is exercised; a blessing comes to each one; if faith asks it shall receive; if hope seeks it shall find; and if love knocks it shall be opened to her.

These three modes of prayer suit us in different stages of distress. There am I, a poor mendicant at mercy's door, I ask, and I shall receive: but I lose my way, so that I cannot find Him of Whom I once asked so successfully; well then I may seek with the certainty that I shall find; and if I am in the last stage of all, not merely poor and bewildered, but so defiled as to feel shut out from God, like a leper shut out of the camp, then I may knock and the door will open to me.

Each one of these different descriptions of prayer is exceedingly simple. If anybody said "I cannot ask," our reply would be, you do not understand the word. Surely everybody can ask. A little child can ask. Long before an infant can speak it can ask—it need not use words in order to ask for what it wants, and there is not one among us who is incapacitated from asking. Prayers need not be fine. I believe God abhors fine prayers. When we pray, the simpler our prayers are the better; the plainest, humblest language which expresses our meaning is the best.

The next word is *seek*, and surely there is no difficulty about seeking? In finding there might be, but in seeking there is none. When the woman in the parable lost her money, she lit a candle and sought for it. I do not suppose she had ever been to the university, or qualified as a lady physician, or that she could have sat on the School Board as a woman of superior sense—but she could seek. Anybody who desires to do so can seek, be they man, woman, or child; and for their encouragement the promise is not given to some particular philosophical form of seeking, but "he that seeketh findeth."

Then there is *knocking* : well, that is a thing of no great difficulty. We used to do it when we were boys, sometimes too much for the neighbours' comfort; and at home, if the knocker was a little too high, we had ways and means of knocking at the door even then; a stone would do it, or the heel of a boot, anything would make a knocking: it was not beyond our capacity by any means. Therefore, it is put in this fashion by Christ himself, as much as to tell us, "Ye need have no scholarship, no training, no talent, and no wit for prayer; ask, seek, knock, that is all, and the promise is to everyone of these ways of praying."

Will you believe the promise? It is Christ who gives it. No lie ever fell from His lips. O doubt Him not. Pray on if you have prayed, and if you have never prayed before, God help you to begin to-day!

III. Our third point is that JESUS TESTIFIES TO THE FACT THAT PRAYER IS HEARD. Having given a promise He then adds, in effect—"You may be quite sure that this promise will be fulfilled, not only because I say it, but because it is and always has been so." When a man says the sun will rise to-morrow morning, we believe it because it always has risen. Our Lord tells us that, as a matter of indisputable fact, all along the ages true asking has been followed by receiving. Remember that he who stated this fact knew it. If you state a fact you may reply, "Yes, as far as your observation goes, it is true," but the observation of Christ was unbounded. There was never a true prayer offered unknown to Him. Prayers acceptable with the Most High come up to Him by the way of the wounds of Christ. Hence the Lord Jesus Christ can speak by personal knowledge, and His declaration is that prayer has succeeded: "Everyone that asketh receiveth, and he that seeketh findeth."

Now here we must, of course, suppose the limitations which would be made by ordinary common sense, and which are made by Scripture. It is not every one that frivolously or wickedly asks or pretends to ask of God that gets what he asks for. It is not every silly, idle, unconsidered request of unregenerate hearts that God will answer. By no manner of means—common sense limits the statement so far. Besides, Scripture limits it again. "Ye have not because ye ask not, or because ye ask amiss"—there is an asking amiss which will never obtain. But those things being remembered, the statement of our Lord has no other qualification—"Every one that asketh receiveth."

Let it be remembered that frequently even when the ungodly and the wicked have asked of God they have received. Full often in the time of their distress they have called upon God, and He has answered them. "Say you so?" saith one. Nay, I say not so,

but so saith Scripture. Ahab's prayer was answered, and the
Lord said, "seest thou how Ahab humbleth himself before me?
because he humbleth himself before me, I will not bring the evil
in his days: but in his son's days will I bring the evil upon his
house." So, also, the Lord heard the prayer of Jehoahaz, the son
of Jehu, who did evil in the sight of the Lord. 2 Kings xiii. 1—4.
The Israelites also, when for their sins they were given over to their
foes, cried to God for deliverance, and they were answered, yet
the Lord Himself testified concerning them that they did but
flatter with their mouth.

Does this stagger you? Does He not hear the young ravens
when they cry? Do you think He will not hear man, that is formed
in His own image? Do you doubt it? Remember Nineveh. The
prayers offered at Nineveh, were they spiritual prayers? Did
you ever hear of a church of God in Nineveh? I have not, neither
do I believe the Ninevites were ever visited by converting grace;
but they were by the preaching of Jonah convinced that they were
in danger from the great Jehovah, and they proclaimed a fast,
and humbled themselves, and God heard their prayer, and
Nineveh for a while was preserved. Many a time in the hour
of sickness, and in the time of woe, God has heard the prayers of
the unthankful and the evil. Dost thou think God gives nothing
except to the good? Hast thou dwelt at the foot of Sinai and
learned to judge according to the law of merit? What wast thou
when thou didst begin to pray? Wert thou good and righteous?
Has not God commanded thee to do good to the evil? Will He
command thee to do what He will not do Himself? Has He not
said that He "sendeth rain upon the just and upon the unjust,"
and is it not so? Is he not daily blessing those who curse Him,
and doing good to those who despitefully use Him? This is one
of the glories of God's grace; and when there is nothing else good
in the man, yet if there be a cry lifted up from his heart the Lord
deigns full often to send relief from trouble. Now, if God has
heard the prayers even of men who have not sought Him in the
highest manner, and has given them temporary deliverances
in answer to their cries, will He not much more hear you when
you are humbling yourself in His sight, and desiring to be recon-
ciled to Him. Surely there is an argument here.

But to come more fully to the point with regard to real and
spiritual prayers, every one that asketh receiveth without any
limit whatever. There has never been an instance yet of a man
really seeking spiritual blessings of God without his receiving
them. The publican stood afar off, and so broken was his heart that
he dared not look up to heaven, yet God looked down on him.
Manasseh lay in the low dungeon, he had been a cruel persecutor

F

of the saints; there was nothing in him that could commend him to God; but God heard him out of the dungeon, and brought him forth to liberty of soul. Jonah had by his own sin brought himself into the whale's belly, and he was a petulant servant of God at the best, but out of the belly of hell he cried and God heard him. "Every one that asketh receiveth, and he that seeketh findeth, and to him that knocketh it shall be opened." *Every one.* If I wanted evidence I should be able to find it in this tabernacle. I would ask anyone here who has found Christ, to bear witness that God heard his prayer. I do not believe that among the damned in hell there is one who dare say "I sought the Lord and He rejected me."

There shall not be found at the last day of account, one single soul that can say, "I knocked at mercy's door, but God refused to open it." There shall not stand before the great white throne, a single soul that can plead, "O Christ, I would have been saved by thee, but thou wouldst not save me. I gave myself up into Thy hands, but Thou didst reject me. I penitently asked for mercy of Thee, but I had it not." Every one that asketh receiveth. It has been so until this day—it will be so till Christ Himself shall come. If you doubt it try it, and if you have tried it try it again. Are you in rags?—that matters not, *every one* that asketh receiveth. Are you foul with sin?—that signifies not, "*every one* that seeketh findeth." Do you feel yourself as if you were shut out from God altogether?—that matters not either, "knock, and it *shall* be opened unto you, for *every one* that asketh receiveth." "Is there no election there?" Ay, ay, doubtless there is, but that does not alter this truth which has no limit to it whatsoever,—"*every one.*" What a rich text it is! "*Every one* that asketh receiveth."

When our Lord spake thus, He could have pointed to His own life as evidence; at any rate, we can refer to it now and show that no one asked of Christ who did not receive. The Syro-Phœnician woman was at first repulsed when the Lord called her a dog, but when she had the courage to say, "yet the dogs eat the crumbs that fall from the table," she soon discovered that every one that asketh receiveth. She, also, who came behind Him in the press and touched the hem of His garment, she was no asker, but she was a seeker, and she found.

I think I hear, in answer to all this, the lamentable wail of one who says, "I have been crying to God a long while for salvation; I have asked, I have sought, and I have knocked, but it has not come yet." Well, dear friend, if I be asked which is true, God or thou, I know which I shall stand by, and I would advise thee to believe God before thou believest thyself. God will hear prayer, but dost thou know there is one thing before

prayer? What is it? Why, the gospel is not—he that prays shall
be saved, that is not the gospel; I believe he will be saved, but
that is not the gospel I am told to preach to you. "Go ye into
all the world and preach the gospel to every creature; he"—
what?—"he that believeth and is baptised shall be saved."
Now, thou hast been asking God to save thee,—dost thou expect
Him to save thee without thy believing and being baptised?
Surely thou hast not had the impudence to ask God to make
void His own word! Might He not say to thee, "This as I bid
thee, believe My Son: he that believeth on Him hath everlasting
life." Let me ask thee, dost thou believe Jesus Christ? Wilt thou
trust Him? "Oh, I trust Him," saith one, "I trust Him wholly."
Soul, do not ask for salvation any more—you have it already
you are saved. If you trust Jesus with all your soul, your sins are
forgiven you, and you are saved; and the next time you approach
the Lord, go with praise as well as with prayer, and sing and
bless His name.

"But how am I to know that I am saved?" saith one. God
saith, "He that believeth and is baptised, shall be saved." Hast
thou believed, hast thou been baptised? If so, thou art saved
How know I that? On the best evidence in all the world: God
says thou art—dost thou want any evidence but that? "I want
to feel this." Feel! Are thy feelings better than God's witness?
Wilt thou make God a liar by asking more signs and tokens than
His sure word of testimony? I have no evidence this day that I
dare trust in concerning my salvation but this, that I rest on
Christ alone with all my heart, and soul, and strength. "Other
refuge have I none," and if thou hast that evidence it is all the
evidence that thou needest seek for this day. Other witnesses
of grace in thy heart shall come by and by, and cluster about thee,
and adorn the doctrine thou dost profess, but now thy first
business is to believe in Jesus.

"I have asked for faith," says one. Well, what doest thou mean
by that? To believe in Jesus Christ is the gift of God, but it must be
thine own act as well. Dost thou think God will believe for
thee, or that the Holy Ghost believes instead of us? What has the
Holy Spirit to believe? Thou must believe for thyself, or be lost.
He cannot lie, wilt thou not believe in Him? He deserves to be
believed, trust in Him, and thou art saved, and thy prayer is
answered.

I think I hear another say, "I trust I am already saved; but
I have been looking for the salvation of others in answer to my
prayers"; Dear friend, you will get it. "He that asketh receiveth;
and he that seeketh findeth; and to him that knocketh it shall
be opened." "But I have sought the conversion of such an one

for years with many prayers." Thou shalt have it, or thou shalt
know one day why thou hast it not, and shall be made content
not to have it. Pray on in hope. Many a one has had his prayer
for others answered after he had been dead. I think I have
reminded you before of the father who had prayed for many
years for his sons and daughters, and yet they were not converted,
but all became exceedingly worldly. His time came to die.
He gathered his children about his bed, hoping to bear such a
witness for Christ at the last that it might be blessed to their
conversion; but unhappily for him he was in deep distress of soul,
he had doubts about his own interest in Christ. He was one of
God's children who are put to bed in the dark; this being above
all the worst fear of his mind, that he feared his dear children
would see his distress and be prejudiced against religion. The
good man was buried and his sons came to the funeral, and God
heard the man's prayer that very day, for as they went away
from the grave one of them said to the other, "Brother, our father
died a most unhappy death." "He did, brother; I was very
much astonished at it, for I never knew a better man than our
father." "Ah," said the first brother, "if a holy man such as
our father found it a hard thing to die, it will be a dreadful
thing for us who have no faith when our time comes." That
same thought had struck them all, and drove them to the cross,
and so the good man's prayer was heard in a mysterious manner.
Heaven and earth shall pass away, but while God lives, prayer
must be heard. While God remains true to His word, supplication
is not in vain. The Lord give you grace to exercise it continually.
Amen.

EJACULATORY PRAYER

A Sermon

Text.—"So I prayed to the God of heaven."—Nehemiah ii. 4.

As we have already seen in the reading of the Scripture, Nehemiah had made enquiry as to the state of the city of Jerusalem, and the tidings he heard caused him bitter grief. "Why should not my countenance be sad," he said, "when the city, the place of my fathers' sepulchres, lieth waste, and the gates thereof are consumed with fire?" He could not endure that it should be a mere ruinous heap—that city which was once beautiful for situation and the joy of the whole earth. Laying the matter to heart, he did not begin to speak to other people about what they would do, nor did he draw up a wonderful scheme about what might be done if so many thousand people joined in the enterprise; but it occurred to him that he would do something himself. This is just the way that practical men start a matter. The unpractical will plan, arrange, and speculate about what may be done, but the genuine, thorough-going lover of Zion puts this question to himself—"What can you do? Nehemiah, what can you do yourself? Come, it has to be done, and you are the man that is to do it—at least, to do your share. What can you do?"

Coming so far, he resolved to set apart a time for prayer. He never had it off his mind for nearly four months. Day and night Jerusalem seemed written on his heart, as if the name were painted on his eyeballs. He could only see Jerusalem. When he slept he dreamed about Jerusalem. When he woke, the first thought was "Poor Jerusalem!" and before he fell asleep again his evening prayer was for the ruined walls of Jerusalem. The man of one thing, you know, is a terrible man; and when one single passion has absorbed the whole of his manhood something will be sure to come of it. Depend upon that. The desire of his heart will develop into some open demonstration, especially if he talks the matter over before God in prayer. Something did come of this. Before long Nehemiah had an opportunity. Men of God, if you want to serve God and cannot find the propitious occasion, wait awhile in prayer and your opportunity will break on your path like a sunbeam. There was never a true and valiant heart that failed to find a fitting sphere somewhere or other in his service. Every diligent labourer is needed in some part of His vineyard. You may have to linger, you may seem as if you stood in the market idle, because the Master would not engage you, but wait there in prayer, and with your heart boiling over with a warm purpose, and your chance will come. The hour will need its man, and if you are ready, you, as a man, shall not be without your hour.

God sent Nehemiah an opportunity. That opportunity came, 'tis true, in a way which he could not have expected. It came through his own sadness of heart. This matter preyed upon his mind till he began to look exceedingly unhappy. I cannot tell whether others remarked it, but the king whom he served, when he went into court with the royal goblet, noticed the distress on the cupbearer's countenance, and he said to him, "Why is thy countenance sad, seeing thou art not sick? This is nothing else but sorrow of heart." Nehemiah little knew that his prayer was making the occasion for him. The prayer was registering itself upon his face. His fasting was making its marks upon his visage; and, though he did not know it, he was, in that way, preparing the opportunity for himself when he went in before the king. But you see when the opportunity did come there was trouble with it, for he says, "I was very sore afraid." Thereupon the king asks him what he really wishes; by the manner of the question he would seem to imply an assurance that he means to help him. And here we are somewhat surprised to find that, instead of promptly answering the king—the answer is not given immediately—an incident occurs, a fact is related. Though he was a man who had lately given himself up to prayer and fasting, this little parenthesis occurs—"So I prayed to the God of heaven." My preamble leads up to this parenthesis. Upon this prayer I propose to preach. Three thoughts occur to me here, on each of which I intend to enlarge—*the fact that Nehemiah did pray just then ; the manner of his prayer ;* and, *the excellent kind of prayer he used.*

I. THE FACT THAT NEHEMIAH PRAYED CHALLENGES ATTENTION. He had been asked a question by his sovereign. The proper thing you would suppose was to answer it. Not so. Before he answered he prayed to the God of heaven. I do not suppose the king noticed the pause. Probably the interval was not long enough to be noticed, but it was long enough for God to notice it—long enough for Nehemiah to have sought and have obtained guidance from God as to how to frame his answer to the king. Are you not surprised to find a man of God having time to pray to God between a question and an answer? Yet Nehemiah found that time. We are the more astonished at his praying, because he was so evidently perturbed in mind, for, according to the second verse, he was very sore afraid. When you are fluttered and put out you may forget to pray . Do you not, some of you, account it a valid excuse for omitting your ordinary devotion? Nehemiah, however, felt that if he was alarmed it was a reason for praying, not for forgetting to pray. So habitually was he in communion with God that as soon as he found himself in a dilemma he flew away to God, just as the dove would fly to hide herself in the clefts of the rock.

His prayer was the more remarkable on this occasion, because *he must have felt very eager about his object.* The king asks him what it is he wants, and his whole heart is set upon building up Jerusalem. Are not you surprised that he did not at once say, "O king, live for ever. I long to build up Jerusalem's walls. Give me all the help thou canst"? But no, eager as he was to pounce upon the desired object, he withdraws his hand until it is said, "So I prayed to the God of heaven." I confess I admire him. I desire also to imitate him. I would that every Christian's heart might have just that holy caution that did not permit him to make such haste as to find ill-speed. "Prayer and provender hinder no man's journey." Certainly, when the desire of our heart is close before us, we are anxious to seize it; but we shall be all the surer of getting the bird we spy in the bush to be a bird we grasp in the hand if we quietly pause, lift up our heart and pray unto the God of heaven.

It is all the more surprising that he should have deliberately prayed just then, because *he had been already praying for the past three or four months* concerning the selfsame matter. Some of us would have said, "That is the thing I have been praying for; now all I have got to do is to take it and use it. Why pray any more? After all my midnight tears and daily cries, after setting myself apart by fasting to cry unto the God of heaven, after such an anxious conference, surely at last the answer has come. What is to be done but to take the good that God provides me with and rejoice in it?" But no, you will always find that the man who has prayed much is the man to pray more. "For unto every one that hath shall be given, and he shall have abundance." If you do but know the sweet art of prayer, you are the man that will be often engaged in it. If you are familiar with the mercy-seat you will constantly visit it.

> "For who that knows the power of prayer
> But wishes to be often there?"

Although Nehemiah had been praying all this while, he nevertheless must offer another petition. "So I prayed to the God of heaven."

One thing more is worth recollecting, namely, that *he was in a king's palace,* and in the palace of a heathen king, too; and he was in the very act of handing up to the king the goblet of wine. He was fulfilling his part in the state festival, I doubt not, amongst the glare of lamps and the glitter of gold and silver, in the midst of princes and peers of the realm. Or even if it were a private festival with the king and queen only, yet still men generally feel so impressed on such occasions with the responsibility of their high position that they are apt to forget prayer. But this devout Israelite, at such a time and in such a place, when he stands at the king's foot to hold up to him the golden goblet, refrains from answering the king's question until first he has prayed to the God of heaven.

II. There is the fact, and I think it seems to prompt further enquiry. So we pass on to observe—THE MANNER OF THIS PRAYER.

Well, very briefly, it was what we call *ejaculatory prayer*—prayer which, as it were, hurls a dart and then it is done. It was not the prayer which stands knocking at mercy's door—knock, knock, knock; but it was the concentration of many knocks into one. It was begun and completed, as it were, with one stroke. This ejaculatory prayer I desire to commend to you as among the very best forms of prayer.

Notice, how *very short* it must have been. It was introduced— slipped in—sandwiched in—between the king's question and Nehemiah's answer; and, as I have already said, I do not suppose it took up any time at all that was appreciable—scarcely a second. Most likely the king never observed any kind of pause or hesitation, for Nehemiah was in such a state of alarm at the question that I am persuaded he did not allow any demur or vacillation to appear, but the prayer must have been offered like an electric flash, very rapidly indeed. In certain states of strong excitement it is wonderful how much the mind gets through in a short time. As drowning men when rescued and recovered have been heard to say that while they were sinking they saw the whole panorama of their lives pass before them in a few seconds, so the mind must be capable of accomplishing much in a brief space of time. Thus the prayer was presented like the winking of an eye; it was done intuitively; yet done it was, and it proved to be a prayer that prevailed with God.

It was a prayer of a *remarkable kind*. I know it was so, because Nehemiah never forgot that he did pray it. I have prayed hundreds of times, and thousands of times, and not recollected any minute particular afterwards either as to the occasion that prompted or the emotions that excited me; but there are one or two prayers in my life that I never can forget. I have not jotted them down in a diary, but I remember when I prayed, because the time was so special and the prayer was so intense, and the answer to it was so remarkable. Now, Nehemiah's prayer was never, never erased from his memory; and when these words of history were written down he wrote that down, "So I prayed to the God of heaven."

III. Now, beloved friends, I come, in the third place to recommend to you THIS EXCELLENT STYLE OF PRAYING.

I shall speak to the children of God mainly, to you that have faith in God. I beg you often, nay, I would ask you always to use this method of ejaculatory prayer. And I would to God, also, that some here who have never prayed before would offer an ejaculation to the God of heaven before they leave this house— that a short but fervent petition, something like that of the publican in the temple, might go up from you—"God be merciful to me a sinner."

To deal with this matter practically, then, *it is the duty and privilege of every Christian to have set times of prayer*. I cannot understand a man's keeping up the vitality of godliness unless he regularly retires for prayer, morning and evening at the very least. Daniel prayed three times a day, and David says, "Seven times a day will I praise thee." It is good for your hearts, good for your memory, good for your moral consistency that you should hedge about certain portions of time and say, "These belong to God. I shall do business with God at such-and-such a time, and try to be as punctual to my hours with him as I should be if I made an engagement to meet a friend." When Sir Thomas Abney was Lord Mayor of London the banquet somewhat troubled him, for Sir Thomas always had prayer with his family at a certain time. The difficulty was how to quit the banquet to keep up family devotion; but so important did he consider it that he vacated the chair, saying to a person near that he had a special engagement with a dear friend which he must keep. And he did keep it, and he returned again to his place, none of the company being the wiser, but he himself being all the better for observing his wonted habit of worship. Mrs. Rowe used to say that when her time came for prayer she would not give it up if the apostle Paul were preaching. Nay, she said, if all the twelve apostles were there, and could be heard at no other time, she would not absent herself from her closet when the set time came round.

But now, having urged the importance of such habitual piety, I want to impress on you the value of another sort of prayer; namely, *the short, brief, quick, frequent ejaculations* of which Nehemiah gives us a specimen. And I recommend this, because it hinders no engagement and occupies no time. You may be measuring off your calicoes, or weighing your groceries, or you may be casting up an account, and between the items you may say,

"Lord, help me." You may breathe a prayer to heaven and say, "Lord, keep me." It will take no time. It is one great advantage to persons who are hard pressed in business that such prayers as those will not, in the slightest degree, incapacitate them from attending to the business they may have in hand. It requires you to go to no particular place. You can stand where you are, ride in a cab, walk along the streets, be the bottom sawyer in a saw pit, or the top one either and yet pray just as well such prayers as these. No altar, no church, no so-called sacred place is needed, but wherever you are, just such a little prayer as that will reach the ear of God, and win a blessing.

Such a prayer as that can be offered anywhere, under any circumstances. On the land, or on the sea, in sickness or in health, amidst losses or gains, great reverses or good returns, still might he breathe his soul in short, quick sentences to God. The advantage of such a way of praying is that you can pray often and pray always. The habit of prayer is blessed, but the spirit of prayer is better; and the spirit of prayer it is which is the mother of these ejaculations; and therefore do I like them, because she is a plentiful mother. Many times in a day may we speak with the Lord our God.

Such prayer may be suggested by all sorts of surroundings. I recollect a poor man once paying me a compliment which I highly valued at the time. He was lying in a hospital, and when I called to see him he said, "I heard you for some years, and now whatever I look at seems to remind me of something or other that you said, and it comes back to me as fresh as when I first heard it." Well, now, he that knows how to pray ejaculatory prayers will find everything about him helping him to the sacred habit. Is it a beautiful landscape? Say, "Blessed be God who has strewn these treasures of form and colour through the world, to cheer the sight and gladden the heart." Are you in doleful darkness, and is it a foggy day? Say, "Lighten my darkness, O Lord." Are you in the midst of company? You will be reminded to pray, "Lord, keep the door of my lips." Are you quite alone? Then can you say, "Let me not be alone, but be thou with me, Father." The putting on of your clothes, the sitting at the breakfast table, the getting into the conveyance, the walking the streets, the opening of your ledger, the putting up of your shutters—everything may suggest such prayer as that which I am trying to describe if you be but in the right frame of mind for offering it.

These prayers are commendable, *because they are truly spiritual.* Wordy prayers may also be windy prayers. There is much of praying by book that has nothing whatever to recommend it.

When you have found the benefit of a manual of French conversation to anyone travelling in France without a knowledge of the language, then try how much good a manual of prayers will do a poor soul who does not know how to ask our heavenly Father for a boon or benefit that he needs. *A manual*, a handbook, forsooth! Tush! Pray with your heart, not with your hands. Or, if you would lift hands in prayer, let them be your own hands, not another man's. The prayers that come leaping out of the soul—the gust of strong emotion, fervent desire, lively faith—these are the truly spiritual; and no prayers but spiritual prayers will God accept.

This kind of prayer is free from any suspicion that it is prompted by the corrupt motive of being offered to please men. They cannot say that the secret ejaculations of our soul are presented with any view to our own praise, for no man knows that we are praying at all; therefore do I commend such prayers to you, and hope that you may abound therein. There have been hypocrites that have prayed by the hour. I doubt not there are hypocrites as regular at their devotions as the angels are before the throne of God, and yet is there no life, no spirit, no acceptance in their pretentious homage; but he that ejaculates—whose heart talks with God—he is no hypocrite. There is a reality, and force, and life about it. If I see sparks come out of a chimney I know there is a fire inside somewhere, and ejaculatory prayers are like the sparks that fly from a soul that is filled with burning coals of love to Jesus Christ.

Short, ejaculatory prayers are of great use to us, dear friends. Often-times they check us. Bad-tempered people, if you were always to pray just a little before you let angry expressions fly from your lips, why many times you would not say those naughty words at all. They advised a good woman to take a glass of water and hold some of it in her mouth five minutes before she scolded her husband. I dare say it was not a bad recipe, but if, instead of practising that little eccentricity, she would just breathe a short prayer to God, it would certainly be more effectual, and far more scriptural. I can recommend it as a valuable prescription for the hasty and the peevish; for all who are quick to take offence and slow to forgive insult or injury. When in business you are about to close in with an offer about the propriety of which you have a little doubt, or a positive scruple, such a prayer as "Guide me, good Lord" would often keep you back from doing what you will afterwards regret.

The habit of offering these brief prayers would also check your confidence in yourself. It would show your dependence upon God. It would keep you from getting worldly. It would be like sweet perfume burnt in the chamber of your soul to keep away the fever of the world from your heart. I can strongly recommend these short, sweet, blessed prayers. May the Holy Ghost give them to you!

Besides, they *actually bring us blessings from heaven*. Ejaculatory prayers, as in the case of Eliezer, the servant of Abraham as in the case of Jacob when he said even in dying, "I have waited for thy salvation, O God,"—prayers such as Moses offered when we do not read that he prayed at all, and yet God said to him, Why cryest thou unto me; ejaculations such as David frequently presented, these were all successful with the Most High. Therefore abound in them, for God loves to encourage and to answer them.

I might thus keep on recommending ejaculatory prayer, but I will say one more thing in its favour. I believe it is very suitable to some persons of a peculiar temperament who could not pray for a long time to save their lives. Their minds are rapid and quick. Well, dear friends, time is not an element in the business, God does not hear us because of the length of our prayer, but because of the sincerity of it. Prayer is not to be measured by the yard, nor weighed by the pound. It is the might and force of it— the truth and reality of it—the energy and the intensity of it. You that are either of so little a mind or of so quick a mind that you cannot use many words, or continue long to think of one thing, it should be to your comfort that ejaculatory prayers are acceptable. And it may be, dear friend, that you are in a condition of body in which you cannot pray any other way. A headache such as some people are frequently affected with the major part of their lives—a state of body which the physician can explain to you— might prevent the mind from concentrating itself long upon one subject. Then it is refreshing to be able again and again and again —fifty or a hundred times a day—to address one's self to God in short, quick sentences, the soul being all on fire. This is a blessed style of praying.

Now, I shall conclude by just mentioning a few of the times *when* I think we ought to resort to this practice of ejaculatory prayer. Mr. Rowland Hill was a remarkable man for the depth of his piety, but when I asked at Wotton-under-Edge for his study, though I rather pressed the question, I did not obtain a satisfactory reply. At length the good minister said, "The fact is, we never found any. Mr. Hill used to study in the garden, in the parlour, in the bed-room, in the streets, in the woods, anywhere." "But where did he retire for prayer?" They said they supposed it was in his chamber, but that he was always praying—that it did not matter where he was, the good old man was always praying. It seemed as if his whole life, though he spent it in the midst of his fellow-men doing good, was passed in perpetual prayer. He had been known to stand in the Blackfriars' road, with his hands under his coat tails, looking in a shop window, and if you listened you might soon perceive that he was breathing out his soul before God. He had got into a constant state of prayer. I believe it is the best condition in which a man can be— praying always, praying without ceasing, always drawing near to God with these ejaculations.

But if I must give you a selection of suitable times I should mention such as these. Whenever you have a great joy, cry, "Lord, make this a real blessing to me." Do not exclaim with others, "Am I not a lucky fellow?" but say, "Lord, give me more grace, and more gratitude, now that thou dost multiply thy favours." When you have got any arduous undertaking on hand or a heavy piece of business, do not touch it till you have breathed your soul out in a short prayer. When you have a difficulty before you, and you are seriously perplexed, when business has got into a tangle or a confusion which you cannot unravel or arrange, breathe a prayer. It need not occupy a minute, but it is wonderful how many snarls come loose after just a word of prayer.

Are the children particularly troublesome to you, good woman? Do you seem as if your patience was almost worn out with the worry and harass? Now for an ejaculatory prayer. You will manage them all the better, and you will bear with their naught tempers all the more quietly. At any rate your own mind will be the less ruffled. Do you think that there is a temptation before you? Do you begin to suspect that somebody is plotting against you? Now for a prayer, "Lead me in a plain path because of mine enemies." Are you at work at the bench, or in a shop, or a warehouse, where lewd conversation and shameful blasphemies assail your ears? Now for a short prayer. Have you noticed some sin that grieves you? Let it move you to prayer. These things ought to remind you to pray. I believe the devil would not let people swear so much if Christian people always prayed every time they heard an oath. He would then see it did not pay. Their blasphemies might somewhat be hushed if they provoked us to supplication.

Do you feel your own heart going off the lines? Does sin begin to fascinate you? Now for a prayer—a warm, earnest, passionate cry, "Lord, hold thou me up." Did you see something with your eye, and did that eye infect your heart? Do you feel as if "your feet were almost gone, and your steps had well nigh slipped?" Now for a prayer—"Hold me, Lord, by my right hand." Has something quite unlooked for happened? Has a friend treated you badly? Then like David say, "Lord, put to nought the counsel of Ahithophel." Breathe a prayer now. Are you anxious to do some good? Be sure to have a prayer over it. Do you mean to speak to that young man as he goes out of the Tabernacle to-night about his soul? Pray first, brother. Do you mean to address yourself to the members of your class and write them a letter this week about their spiritual welfare? Pray over every line, brother. It is always good to have praying going on while you are talking about Christ. I always find I can preach the better if I can pray while I am preaching.

And the mind is very, remarkable in its activities. It can be praying while it is studying: it can be looking up to God while it is talking to man; and there can be one hand held up to receive supplies from God while the other hand is dealing out the same supplies which He is pleased to give. Pray as long as you live. Pray when you are in great pain; the sharper the pang then the more urgent and importunate should your cry to God be. And when the shadow of death gathers round you, and strange feelings flush or chill you, and plainly tell that you near the journey's end, then pray. Oh! that is a time for ejaculation. Short and pithy prayers like this: "Hide not thy face from me, O Lord"; or this, "Be not far from me, O God"; will doubtless suit you. "Lord Jesus, receive my spirit," were the thrilling words of Stephen in his extremity; and "Father, into thy hands I commend my spirit," were the words that your Master Himself uttered just before He bowed His head and gave up the ghost. You may well take up the same strain and imitate Him.

These thoughts and counsels are so exclusively addressed to the saints and faithful brethren in Christ that you will be prone to ask, "Is not there anything to be said to the unconverted?" Well, whatever has been spoken in their hearing may be used by them for their own benefit. But let me address myself to you, my dear friends, as pointedly as I can. Though you are not saved, yet you must not say, "I cannot pray." Why, if prayer is thus simply, what excuse can you have for neglecting it? It wants no measurable space of time. Such prayers as these God will hear, and ye have all of you the ability and opportunity to think and to express them, if you have only that elementary faith in God which believes "that he is, and that he is a rewarder of them that diligently seek him." Cornelius had, I suppose, got about as far as this, when he was admonished by the angel to send for Peter, who preached to him peace by Jesus Christ to the conversion of his soul. Is there such a strange being in the Tabernacle to-night as a man or woman that never prays? How shall I expostulate with you? May I steal a passage from a living poet who, though he has contributed nothing to our hymn books, hums a note so suited to my purpose, and so pleasant to my ear that I like to quote it—

" More things are wrought by prayer
Than this world dreams of. Wherefore let thy voice
Rise like a fountain, flowing night and day:
For what are men better than sheep or goats,
That nourish a blind life within the brain,
If, knowing God, they lift not hands of prayer,
Both for themselves and those who call them friend?
For so the whole round world is every way
Bound by gold chains about the feet of God."

I do not suspect there is a creature here who never prays, because people generally pray to somebody or other. The man that never prays to God such prayers as he ought, prays to God such prayers as he ought not. It is an awful thing when a man asks God to damn him; and yet there are persons that do that. Suppose He were to hear you; He is a prayer-hearing God. If I address one profane swearer here I would like to put this matter clearly to him. Were the Almighty to hear you. If your eyes were blinded and your tongue were struck dumb while you were uttering a wild imprecation, how would you bear the sudden judgment on your impious speech? If some of those prayers of yours were answered for yourself, and some that you have offered in your passion for your wife and for your child, were fulfilled to their hurt and your distraction, what an awful thing it would be. Well, God does answer prayer, and one of these days He may answer your prayers to your shame and everlasting confusion. Would not it be well now, before you leave your seat, to pray, "Lord have mercy upon me; Lord, save me; Lord, change my heart; Lord, give me to believe in Christ; Lord, give me now an interest in the precious blood of Jesus; Lord, save me now?" Will not each one of you breathe such a prayer as that? May the Holy Spirit lead you so to do, and if you once begin to pray aright I am not afraid that you will ever leave off, for there is a something that holds the soul fast in real prayer. Sham prayers— what is the good of them? But real heart pleading—the soul talking with God—when it once begins will never cease. You will have to pray till you exchange prayer for praise, and go from the mercy-seat below to the throne of God above.

May God bless you all; all of you, I say; all who are my kindred in Christ, and all for whose salvation I yearn. God bless you all and every one, for our dear Redeemer's sake. Amen.

ASK AND HAVE

A Sermon

Text.—"Ye lust, and have not: ye kill, and desire to have, and cannot obtain: ye fight and war, yet ye have not, because ye ask not. Ye ask, and receive not, because ye ask amiss, that ye may consume it upon your lusts."—James iv. 2, 3.

MAY these striking words be made profitable to us by the teaching of the Holy Spirit.

Man is a creature abounding in wants, and ever restless, and hence his heart is full of desires. I can hardly imagine a man existing who has not many desires of some kind or another. Man is comparable to the sea anemone with its multitude of tentacles which are always hunting in the water for food; or like certain plants which send out tendrils, seeking after the means of climbing. The poet says, "Man never is, but always to be, blest." He steers for which he thinks to be his port, but as yet he is tossed about on the waves. One of these days he hopes to find his heart's delight, and so he continues to desire with more or less expectancy.

This fact appertains both to the worst of men and the best of men. In bad men desires corrupt into lusts: they long after that which is selfish, sensual, and consequently evil. The current of their desires set strongly in a wrong direction. These lustings, in many cases, become extremely intense: they make the man their slave; they domineer over his judgment; they stir him up to violence: he fights and wars, perhaps he literally kills: in God's sight, who counts anger murder, he does kill full often. Such is the strength of his desires that they are commonly called passions; and when these passions are fully excited, then the man himself struggles vehemently, so that the kingdom of the devil suffereth violence, and the violent take it by force.

Meanwhile in gracious men there are desires also. To rob the saints of their desires would be to injure them greatly, for by these they rise out of their lower selves. The desires of the gracious are after the best things: things pure and peaceable, laudable and elevating. They desire God's glory, and hence their desires spring from higher motives than those which inflame the unrenewed mind. Such desires in Christian men are frequently very fervent and forcible; they ought always to be so; and those desires begotten of the Spirit of God stir the renewed nature, exciting and stimulating it, and making the man to groan and to be in anguish and in travail until he can attain that which God has taught him to long for. The lusting of the wicked and the holy desiring of the righteous have their own ways of seeking gratification. The lusting of the wicked developes itself in contention; it kills, and desires to have; it fights and it wars; while on the other hand the desire of the righteous when rightly guided betakes itself to a far better course for achieving its purpose, for it expresses itself in prayer fervent and importunate. The godly man when full of desire asks and receives at the hand of God.

At this time I shall by God's help try to set forth from our text, first, *the poverty of lusting*,—"Ye lust and have not." Secondly, I shall sadly show *the poverty of many professing Christians* in spiritual things, especially in their church capacity; they also long for and have not. Thirdly, we shall speak in closing, upon *the wealth wherewith holy desires will be rewarded if we will but use the right means.* If we ask we shall receive.

I. First, consider THE POVERTY OF LUSTING,—"*Ye lust, and have not.*" Carnal lustings, however strong they may be, do not in many cases obtain that which they seek after; as saith the text, "Ye desire to have, and cannot obtain." The man longs to be happy, but he is not; he pines to be great, but he grows meaner every day; he aspires after this and after that which he thinks will content him, but he is still unsatisfied; he is like the troubled sea which cannot rest. One way or another his life is disappointment; he labours as in the very fire, but the result is vanity and vexation of spirit. How can it be otherwise? If we sow the wind, must we not reap the whirlwind, and nothing else? Or, if peradventure the strong lustings of an active, talented, persevering man do give him what he seeks after, yet how soon he loses it. He has it so that he has it not. The pursuit is toilsome, but the possession is a dream. He sits down to eat, and lo! the feast is snatched away, the cup vanishes when it is at his lip. He wins to lose; he builds, and his sandy foundation slips from under his tower, and it lies in ruins. He that conquered kingdoms, died discontented on a lone rock in mid ocean; and he who revived his empire, fell never to rise again. As Jonah's gourd withered in a night, so have empires fallen on a sudden, and their lords have died in exile. So that what men obtain by warring and fighting is an estate with a short lease; the obtaining is so temporary that it still stands true, "they lust, and have not."

Or if such men have gifts and power enough to retain that which they have won, yet in another sense they have it not while they have it, for the pleasure which they looked for in it is not there. They pluck the apple, and it turns out to be one of those Dead Sea apples which crumble to ashes in the hand. The man is rich, but God takes away from him the power to enjoy his

G

wealth. By his lustings and his warrings the licentious man at last obtains the object of his cravings, and after a moment's gratification, he loathes that which he so passionately lusted for. He longs for the tempting pleasure, seizes it, and crushes it by the eager grasp. See the boy hunting the butterfly, which flits from flower to flower, while he pursues it ardently. At last it is within reach, and with his cap he knocks it down; but when he picks up the poor remains, he finds the painted fly spoiled by the act which won it. Thus may it be said of multitudes of the sons of men,—"Ye lust, and have not."

Their poverty is set forth in a threefold manner. "Ye kill, and desire to have, and cannot obtain," "Ye have not, because ye ask not," "Ye ask, and receive not, because ye ask amiss."

If the lusters fail, it is not because they did not set to work to gain their ends; for according to their nature they used the most practical means within their reach, and used them eagerly, too. According to the mind of the flesh the only way to obtain a thing is to fight for it, and James sets this down as the reason of all fighting. "Whence come wars and fightings among you? Come they not hence, even of your lusts that war in your members?" This is the form of effort of which we read, "*Ye fight and war, yet ye have not.*" To this mode of operation men cling from age to age. If a man is to get along in this world they tell me he must contend with his neighbours, and push them from their vantage ground; he must not be particular how *they* are to thrive, but he must mind the main chance on his own account, and take care to rise, no matter how many he may tread upon. He cannot expect to get on if he loves his neighbour as himself. It is a fair fight, and every man must look to himself. Do you think I am satirical? I may be, but I have heard this sort of talk from men who meant it. So they take to fighting, and that fighting is often victorious, for according to the text "*ye kill*"— that is to say, they so fight that they overthrow their adversary, and there is an end of him.

Multitudes of men are living for themselves, competing here and warring there, fighting for their own hand with the utmost perseverance. They have little choice as to how they will do it. Conscience is not allowed to interfere in their transactions, but the old advice rings in their ears, "Get money; get money honestly if you can, but by any means get money." No matter though body and soul be ruined, and others be deluged with misery, fight on, for there is no discharge in this war. Well saith James, "Ye kill, and desire to have, and cannot obtain; ye fight and war, yet ye have not."

When men who are greatly set upon their selfish purposes do

not succeed they may possibly hear that the reason of their non-success is "*Because ye ask not.*" Is, then, success to be achieved by asking? So the text seems to hint, and so the righteous find it. Why doth not this man of intense desires take to asking? The reason is, first, because it is unnatural to the natural man to pray; as well expect him to fly. He despises the idea of supplication. "Pray?" says he. "No, I want to be at work. I cannot waste time on devotions; prayers are not practical, I want to fight my way. While you are praying I shall have beaten my opponent. I go to my counting-house, and leave you to your Bibles and your prayers." He hath no mind for asking of God. He is so proud that he reckons himself to be his own providence; his own right hand and his active arm shall get to him the victory. When he is very liberal in his views he admits that though he does not pray, yet there may be some good in it, for it quiets people's minds, and makes them more comfortable: but as to any answer ever coming to prayer, he scouts the idea, and talks both philosophically and theologically about the absurdity of supposing that God alters his course of conduct out of respect to the prayers of men and women. "Ridiculous," says he, "utterly ridiculous"; and, therefore, in his own great wisdom he returns to his fighting and his warring, for by such means he hopes to attain his end. Yet he obtains not. The whole history of mankind shows the failure of evil lustings to obtain their object.

For a while the carnal man goes on fighting and warring; but by-and-by he changes his mind, for he is ill, or frightened. His purpose is the same, but if it cannot be achieved one way he will try another. If he must ask, well, he will ask; he will become religious, and do good to himself in that way. He finds that some religious people prosper in the world, and that even sincere Christians are by no means fools in business, and, therefore, he will try their plan. And now he comes under the third censure of our text,—"*Ye ask and receive not.*" What is the reason why the man who is the slave of his lusts obtains not his desire, even when he takes to asking? The reason is because his asking is a mere matter of form, his heart is not in his worship. He buys a book containing what are called forms of prayer, and he repeats these, for repeating is easier than praying, and demands no thought.

I have no objection to your using a form of prayer if you pray with it; but I know a great many who do not pray with it, but only repeat the form. Imagine what would come to our families if instead of our children speaking to us frankly when they have any need they were always to think it requisite to go into the library and hunt up a form of prayer, and read it to us. Surely there would be an end to all home-feeling and love; life would move in fetters. Our household would become a kind of boarding-school, or barracks, and all would be parade and formality, instead of happy eyes looking up with loving trust into fond eyes that delight to respond. Many spiritual men use a form, but carnal men are pretty sure to do so, for they end in the form.

If your desires are the longings of fallen nature, if your desires begin and end with your own self, and if the chief end for which you live is not to glorify God, but to glorify yourself, then you may fight, but you shall not have; you may rise up early and sit up late, but nothing worth gaining shall come of it. Remember how the Lord hath spoken in the thirty-seventh Psalm: "Cease from anger, and forsake wrath: fret not thyself in any wise to do evil. For yet a little while, and the wicked shall not be: yea, thou shalt diligently consider his place, and it shall not be. But the meek shall inherit the earth; and shall delight themselves in the abundance of peace."

So much upon the poverty of lusting.

II. Secondly, I have now before me a serious business, and that is, to show HOW CHRISTIAN CHURCHES MAY SUFFER SPIRITUAL POVERTY, so that they too "desire to have, and cannot obtain." Of course the Christian seeks higher things than the worldling, else were he not worthy of that name at all. At least professedly his object is to obtain the true riches, and to glorify God in spirit and in truth. Yes, but look, dear brethren, all churches do not get what they desire. We have to complain, not here and there but in many places, of churches that are nearly asleep, and are gradually declining. Of course they find excuses. The population is dwindling, or another place of worship is attracting the people. There is always an excuse handy when a man wants one; but still there stands the fact,—public worship is almost deserted in some places, the ministry has no rallying power about it, and those who put in an appearance are discontented or indifferent. In such churches there are no conversions. And what is the reason of it?

First, *even among professed Christians, there may be the pursuit of desirable things in a wrong method.* "Ye fight and war, yet ye have not." Have not churches thought to prosper by competing with other churches? At such and such a place of worship they have a very clever man: we must get a clever man, too; in fact, he must be a little cleverer than our neighbour's hero. That is the thing, —a clever man! Ah me, that we should live in an age in which we talk about clever men in preaching the gospel of Jesus Christ! Alas, that this holy service should be thought to depend upon human cleverness!

Churches have competed with each other in architecture, in music, in apparel, and in social status. In some cases there is a measure of bitterness in the rivalry. It is not pleasant to little minds to see other churches prospering more than their own. They may be more earnest than we are, and be doing God's work better, but we are too apt to turn a jealous eye towards them, and we would rather they did not get on quite so well. "Do ye think that the Scripture saith in vain, The spirit that dwelleth in us lusteth to envy?" If we could see a disturbance among them, so that they would break up and be ecclesiastically killed, we would not rejoice. Of course not; but neither should we suffer any deadly sorrow. In some churches an evil spirit lingers. I bring no railing accusation, and, therefore, say no more than this: God will never bless such means and such a spirit; those who give way to them will desire to have, but never obtain.

Meanwhile, what is the reason why they do not have a blessing? The text says, "*Because ye ask not*"; I am afraid there are churches which do not ask. Prayer in all forms is too much neglected. Private prayer is allowed to decay. I shall put it to the conscience of every man how far secret prayer is attended to; and how much of fellowship with God there is in secret among the members of our churches. Certainly its healthy existence is vital to church prosperity. Of family prayer it is more easy to judge, for we can see it. I fear that in these days many have quite given up family prayer. I pray you do not imitate them.

I wish you were all of the same mind as the Scotch labourer who obtained a situation in the house of a wealthy farmer who was known to pay well, and all his friends envied him that he had gone to live in such a service. In a short time he returned to his native village, and when they asked him why he had left his situation, he replied that he "could not live in a house which had no roof to it." A house without prayer is a house without a roof. We cannot expect blessings on your churches if we have none on your families.

As to the congregational prayer, the gathering together in what we call our prayer-meetings, is there not a falling off? In many cases the prayer-meeting is despised, and looked down upon as a sort of second-rate gathering. There are members of churches who are never present, and it does not prick their consciences that they stay away. Some congregations mix up the prayer-meeting with a lecture, so as to hold only one service in the week. I read the other day an excuse for all this: it is said that people are better at home, attending to family concerns. This is idle talk, for who among us wishes people to neglect their domestic concerns? It will be found that those attend to their own concerns best who are diligent to get everything in order, so that they may go out to assemblies for worship. Negligence of the house of God is often an index of negligence of their own houses. They are not bringing their children to Christ, I am persuaded, or they would bring them up to the services. Anyhow, the prayers of the church measure its prosperity. If we restrain prayer we restrain the blessing. Our true success as churches can only be had by asking it of the Lord. Are we not prepared to reform and amend in this matter? Oh for Zion's travailing hour to come, when an agony of prayer shall move the whole body of the faithful.

But some reply, "There are prayer-meetings, and we do ask for the blessing, and yet it comes not." Is not the explanation to be found in the other part of the text, "*Ye have not, because ye ask amiss*"? When prayer-meetings become a mere form, when brethren stand up and waste the time with their long orations, instead of speaking to God in earnest and burning words, when there is no expectation of a blessing, when the prayer is cold and chill, then nothing will come of it. He who prays without fervency does not pray at all. We cannot commune with God, who is a consuming fire, if there is no fire in our prayers. Many prayers fail of their errand because there is no faith in them. Prayers which are filled with doubt, are requests for refusal. Imagine that you wrote to a friend and said, "Dear friend, I am in great trouble, and I therefore tell you, and ask for your help, because it seems right to do so. But though I thus write, I have no belief that you will send me any help; indeed, I should be mightily surprised if you did, and should speak of it as a great wonder."

Will you get the help, think you? I should say your friend would be sensible enough to observe the little confidence which you have in him; and he would reply that, as you did not expect anything, he would not astonish you. Your opinion of his generosity is so low that he does not feel called upon to put himself out of the way on your account. When prayers are of that kind you cannot wonder if we "have not, because we ask amiss." Moreover, if our praying, however earnest and believing it may be, is a mere asking that our church may prosper because we want to glory in its prosperity, if we want to see our own denomination largely increased, and its respectability improved, that we may share the honours thereof, then our desires are nothing but lustings after all. Can it be that the children of God manifest the same emulations, jealousies, and ambitions as men of the world? Shall religious work be a matter of rivalry and contest? Ah, then, the prayers which seek success will have no acceptance at the mercy-seat. God will not hear us, but bid us begone, for he careth not for the petitions of which self is the object. "Ye have not, because ye ask not, or because ye ask amiss."

III.   Thirdly, I have a much more pleasing work to do, and that is to hint at THE WEALTH WHICH AWAITS THE USE OF THE RIGHT MEANS, namely, of asking rightly of God.

I invite your most solemn attention to this matter, for it is vitally important. And my first observation is this, *how very small after all is this demand which God makes of us.* Ask! Why, it is the least thing he can possibly expect of us, and it is no more than we ordinarily require of those who need help from us. We expect a poor man to ask; and if he does not we lay the blame of his lack upon himself. If God will give for the asking, and we remain poor, who is to blame? Is not the blame most grievous? Does it not look as if we were out of order with God, so that we will not even condescend to ask a favour of him? Surely there must be in our hearts a lurking enmity to him, or else instead of its being an unwelcome necessity it would be regarded as a great delight.

However, brethren, whether we like it or not, remember, *asking is the rule of the kingdom.* "Ask, and ye shall receive." It is a rule that never will be altered in anybody's case. Our Lord Jesus Christ is the elder brother of the family, but God has not relaxed the rule for Him. Remember this text: Jehovah says to His own Son, "Ask of me and I will give thee the heathen for thine inheritance, and the uttermost parts of the earth for thy possession." If the royal and divine Son of God cannot be exempted from the rule of asking that he may have, you and I cannot expect the rule to be relaxed in our favour. God will bless Elijah and send rain on Israel, but Elijah must pray for it. If the chosen nation is to prosper Samuel must plead for it. If the Jews are to be delivered Daniel must intercede. God will bless Paul, and the nations shall be converted through him, but Paul must pray. Pray he did without ceasing; his epistles show that he expected nothing except by asking for it.

Moreover, it is clear to even the most shallow thinker that *there are some things necessary for the church of God which we cannot get otherwise than by prayer.* You can get that clever man I spoke about; and that new church, and the new organ, and the choir, you can also get without prayer; but you cannot get the heavenly anointing: the gift of God is not to be purchased with money. Some of the members of a church in a primitive village in America thought that they would raise a congregation by hanging up a very handsome chandelier in the meeting-house. People talked about this chandelier, and some went to see it, but the light of it soon grew dim. You can buy all sorts of ecclesiastical furniture, you can purchase any kind of paint, brass, muslin, blue, scarlet, and fine linen, together with flutes, harps, sackbuts, psalteries, and all kinds of music—you can get these without prayer; in fact, it would be an impertinence to pray about such rubbish; but you cannot get the Holy Ghost without prayer. "He bloweth where he listeth." He will not be brought near by any process or method at our command apart from asking. There are no mechanical means which will make up for His absence. Prayer is the great door of spiritual blessing, and if you close it you shut out the favour.

Beloved brethren, do you not think that *this asking which God requires is a very great privilege?* Suppose there were an edict published that you must not pray: that would be a hardship indeed. If prayer rather interrupted than increased the stream of blessing, it would be a sad calamity. Did you ever see a dumb man under a strong excitement, or suffering great pain, and therefore anxious to speak? It is a terrible sight to see: the face is distorted, the body is fearfully agitated; the mute writhes and labours in dire distress. Every limb is contorted with a desire to help the tongue, but it cannot break its bonds. Hollow sounds come from the breast, and stutterings of ineffectual speech awaken attention, though they cannot reach so far as expression. The poor creature is in pain unspeakable. Suppose we were in our spiritual nature full of strong desires, and yet dumb as to the tongue of prayer, methinks it would be one of the direst afflictions that could possibly befall us; we should be terribly maimed and dismembered, and our agony would be overwhelming. Blessed be His name, the Lord ordains a way of utterance, and bids our heart speak out to Him.

Beloved, we must pray: it seems to me that *it ought to be the first thing* we ever think of doing when in need. If men were right with God, and loved Him truly, they would pray as naturally as they breathe. I hope some of us are right with God, and do not need to be driven to prayer, for it has become an instinct of our nature. I was told by a friend yesterday the story of a little German boy; a story which his pastor loved to tell. The dear little child believed his God, and delighted in prayer. His schoolmaster had urged the scholars to be at school in time, and this child always tried to be so; but his father and mother were dilatory people, and one morning, through their fault alone, he had just left the door as the clock struck the hour for the school to open. A friend standing near heard the little one cry, "Dear God, do grant I may be in time for school." It struck the listener that for once prayer could not be heard, for the child had quite a little walk before him, and the hour was already come. He

was curious to see the result. Now it so happened this morning
that the master, in trying to open the schoolhouse door turned
the key the wrong way, and could not stir the bolt, and they had
to send for a smith to open the door. Hence a delay, and just
as the door opened our little friend entered with the rest, all in
good time. God has many ways of granting right desires. It
was most natural that instead of crying and whining a child
that really loved God should speak to Him about his trouble.
Should it not be natural to you and to me spontaneously and at
once to tell the Lord our sorrows and ask for help? Should not
this be the first resort?

Alas, according to Scripture and observation, and I grieve to
add, according to experience, *prayer is often the last thing*. Look
at the sick man in the one hundred and seventh Psalm. Friends
bring him various foods, but his soul abhorreth all manner of
meat: the physicians do what they can to heal him, but he grows
worse and worse, and draws nigh to the gates of death: "Then
they cry unto the Lord in their trouble." That was put last which
should have been first. "Send for the doctor. Prepare him
nourishment. Wrap him in flannels!" All very well, but when
will you pray to God? God will be called upon when the case
grows desperate. Look at the mariners described in the same
psalm. The barque is well-nigh wrecked. "They mount up to
the heaven, they go down again to the depths: their soul is melted
because of trouble." Still they do all they can to ride out the
storm; but when "they reel to and fro, and stagger like a drunken
man, and are at their wit's end: then they cry unto the Lord in
their trouble." Oh, yes; God is sought unto when we are driven
into a corner and ready to perish. And what a mercy it is that
He hears such laggard prayers, and delivers the suppliants out
of their troubles. But ought it to be so with you and with me,
and with churches of Christ? Ought not the first impulse of a
declining church to be, "Let us pray day and night until the
Lord appears for us: let us meet together with one accord in one
place, and never separate until the blessing descends upon us"?

Do you know, brothers, *what great things are to be had for the
asking?* Have you ever thought of it? Does it not stimulate you
to pray fervently? All heaven lies before the grasp of the asking
man; all the promises of God are rich and inexhaustible, and
their fulfilment is to be had by prayer. Jesus saith, "All things
are delivered unto me of my Father," and Paul says, "All things
are yours, and ye are Christ's." Who would not pray when all
things are thus handed over to us? Ay, and promises that were
first made to special individuals, are all made to us if we know
how to plead them in prayer. Israel went through the Red Sea

ages ago, and yet we read in the sixty-sixth Psalm, "There did we rejoice in him." Only Jacob was present at Peniel, and yet Hosea says "There he spake with us."

Paul wants to give us a great promise for times of need, and he quotes from the Old Testament, "For he hath said, I will never leave thee nor forsake thee." Where did Paul get that? That is the assurance which the Lord gave to Joshua: "I will never leave thee nor forsake thee." Surely the promise was for Joshua only. No; it is for us. "No Scripture is of private interpretation"; all Scripture is ours. See how God appears unto Solomon at night, and he says, "Ask what I shall give thee." Solomon asks for wisdom. "Oh, that is Solomon," say you. Listen. "If any man lack wisdom, let him ask of God." God gave Solomon wealth, and fame into the bargain. Is not that peculiar to Solomon? No, for it is said of the true wisdom, "Length of days is in her right hand, and in her left hand riches and honour"; and is not this much like our Saviour's word, "Seek ye first the kingdom of God and his righteousness, and all these things shall be added unto you." Thus you see the Lord's promises have many fulfilments, and they are waiting now to pour their treasures into the lap of prayer. Does not this lift prayer up to a high level, when God is willing to repeat the biographies of His saints in us; when He is waiting to be gracious, and to load us with His benefits?

I will mention another truth which ought to make us pray, and that is, that *if we ask, God will give to us much more than we ask.* Abraham asked of God that Ishmael might live before him. He thought "Surely this is the promised seed: I cannot expect that Sarah will bear a child in her old age. God has promised me a seed, and surely it must be this child of Hagar. Oh that Ishmael might live before thee." God granted him that, but He gave him Isaac as well, and all the blessings of the covenant. There is Jacob, he kneels down to pray, and asks the Lord to give him bread to eat and raiment to put on. But what did his God give him? When he came back to Bethel he had two bands, thousands of sheep and camels, and much wealth. God had heard him and done exceeding abundantly above what he asked. It is said of David, "The king asked life of thee, and thou gavest him length of days," yea, gave him not only length of days himself, but a throne for his sons throughout all generations, till David went in and sat before the Lord, overpowered with the Lord's goodness.

"Well," say you, "but is that true of New Testament prayers?" Yes, it is so with the New Testament pleaders, whether saints or sinners. They brought a man to Christ sick of the palsy, and asked Him to heal him, and He said, "Son, thy sins be forgiven thee." He had not asked that, had he? No, but God gives greater things than we ask for. Hear that poor, dying thief's humble prayer, "Lord, remember me when thou comest into thy kingdom." Jesus replies, "To-day shalt thou be with me in Paradise." He had not dreamed of such an honour. Even the story of the Prodigal teaches us this. He resolved to say, "I am not worthy to be called thy son; make me as one of thy hired servants." What is the answer? "This my son was dead, and is alive again: bring forth the best robe and put it on him; put a ring on his hands, and shoes on his feet." Once get into the position of an asker, and you shall have what you never asked for, and never thought to receive. The text is often misquoted: "God is able to do exceeding abundantly above all that we *can* ask, or even think." We *could* ask, if we were but more sensible and had more faith, for the very greatest things, but God is willing to give us infinitely more than we do ask.

At this moment I believe that God's church might have inconceivable blessings if she were but ready now to pray. Did you ever notice that wonderful picture in the eighth chapter of the Revelation? It is worthy of careful notice. I shall not attempt to explain it in its connection, but merely point to the picture as it hangs on the wall by itself. Read on —"When he had opened the seventh seal, there was silence in heaven about the space of half an hour." Silence in heaven: there were no anthems, no hallelujahs, not an angel stirred a wing. Silence in heaven! Can you imagine it? And look! You see seven angels standing before God, and to them are given seven trumpets. There they wait, trumpet in hand, but there is no sound. Not a single note of cheer or warning during an interval which was sufficiently long to provoke lively emotion, but short enough to prevent impatience. Silence unbroken, profound, awful reigned in heaven. Action is suspended in heaven, the centre of all activity. "And another angel came and stood at the altar, having a golden censer." There he stands, but no offering is presented: everything has come to a standstill. What can possibly set it in motion? "And there was given unto him much incense, that he should offer it with the prayers of all saints upon the golden altar which was before the throne." Prayer is presented together with the merit of the Lord Jesus.

Now, see what will happen. "And the smoke of the incense, which came with the prayers of the saints, ascended up before God out of the angel's hands." That is the key of the whole matter. Now you will see: the angel begins to work: he takes the censer, fills it with the altar fire, and flings it down upon the earth, "and there were voices, and thunderings, and lightnings, and an earthquake." "And the seven angels which had the seven trumpets prepared themselves to sound." Everything is moving now. As soon as the prayers of the saints were mixed with the incense of Christ's eternal merit, and begun to smoke up from the altar, then prayer became effectual. Down fell the living coals among the sons of men, while the angels of the divine providence, who stood still before, sound their thunderblasts, and the will of the Lord is done. Such is the scene in heaven in a certain measure even to this day. Bring hither the incense. Bring hither the prayers of the saints! Set them on fire with Christ's merits, and on the golden altar let them smoke before the Most High: then shall we see the Lord at work, and His will shall be done on earth as it is in heaven. God send His blessing with these words, for Christ's sake. Amen.

ROBINSON CRUSOE'S TEXT

A Sermon

"Call upon me in the day of trouble; I will deliver thee, and thou shalt glorify me."—Psalm i. 15.

ONE book charmed us all in the days of our youth. Is there a boy alive who has not read it? "Robinson Crusoe" was a wealth of wonders to me: I could have read it over a score times, and never have wearied. I am not ashamed to confess that I can read it even now with ever fresh delight. Robinson and his man Friday, though mere inventions of fiction, are wonderfully real to the most of us. But why am I running on in this way on a Sabbath evening? Is not this talk altogether out of order? I hope not. A passage in that book comes vividly before my recollection to-night as I read my text; and in it I find something more than an excuse. Robinson Crusoe has been wrecked. He is left in the desert island all alone. His case is a very pitiable one. He goes to his bed, and he is smitten with fever. This fever lasts upon him long, and he has no one to wait upon him—none even to bring him a drink of cold water. He is ready to perish. He had been accustomed to sin, and had all the vices of a sailor; but his hard case brought him to think. He opens a Bible which he finds in his chest, and he lights upon this passage, "*Call upon me in the day of trouble: I will deliver thee, and thou shalt glorify me.*" That night he prayed for the first time in his life, and ever after there was in him a hope in God, which marked the birth of the heavenly life.

De Foe, who composed the story, was, as you know, a Presbyterian minister; and though not overdone with spirituality, he knew enough of religion to be able to describe very vividly the experience of a man who is in despair, and who finds peace by casting himself upon his God. As a novelist, he had a keen eye for the probable, and he could think of no passage more likely to impress a poor broken spirit than this. Instinctively he perceived the mine of comfort which lies within these words.

Now I have everybody's attention, and this is one reason why I thus commenced my discourse. But I have a further purpose; for although Robinson Crusoe is not here, nor his man Friday either, yet there may be somebody here very like him, a person who has suffered shipwreck in life, and who has now become a drifting, solitary creature. He remembers better days, but by his sins he has become a castaway, whom no man seeks after. He is here to-night, washed up on shore without a friend, suffering in body, broken in estate, and crushed in spirit. In the midst of a city full of people, he has not a friend, nor one who would wish to own that he has ever known him. He has come to the bare bone of existence now. Nothing lies before him but poverty, misery, and death.

Thus saith the Lord unto thee, my friend, this night, "*Call upon me in the day of trouble : I will deliver thee, and thou shalt glorify me.*" I have the feeling upon me that I shall at this time speak home, God helping me, to some poor burdened spirit. Of what use is comfort to those who are not in distress? The word to-night will be of no avail, and have but little interest in it, to those who have no distress of heart. But, however badly I may speak, those hearts will dance for joy which need the cheering assurance of a gracious God, and are enabled to receive it as it shines forth in this golden text: "*Call upon me in the day of trouble : I will deliver thee, and thou shalt glorify me.*" It is a text which I would have written in stars across the sky, or sounded forth with trumpet at noon from the top of every tower, or printed on every sheet of paper which passes through the post. It should be known and read of all mankind.

Four things suggest themselves to me. May the Holy Ghost bless what I am able to say upon them!

I.   The first observation is not so much in my text alone as in the text and the context. REALISM IS PREFERRED TO RITUALISM. If you will carefully read the rest of the Psalm you will see that the Lord is speaking of the rites and ceremonies of Israel, and He is showing that He has little care about formalities of worship when the heart is absent from them. I think we must read the whole passage: "I will not reprove thee for thy sacrifices or thy burnt offerings, to have been continually before me. I will take no bullock out of thy house, nor he goats out of thy folds. For every beast of the forest is mine, and the cattle upon a thousand hills. I know all the fowls of the mountains: and the wild beasts of the field are mine. If I were hungry, I would not tell thee: for the world is mine, and the fulness thereof. Will I eat the flesh of bulls, or drink the blood of goats? Offer unto God thanksgiving; and pay thy vows unto the Most High: and call upon me in the day of trouble: I will deliver thee, and thou shalt glorify me." Thus praise and prayer are accepted in preference to every form of offering which it was possible for the Jew to present before the Lord. Why is this?

First of all I would answer, real prayer is far better than mere ritual, because *there is meaning in it*, and when grace is absent, there is no meaning in ritual; it is as senseless as an idiot's game.

Did you ever stand in some Romish cathedral and see the daily service, especially if it happened to be upon a high day? What with the boys in white, and the men in violet, or pink, or red, or black, there were performers enough to stock a decent village. What with those who carried candlesticks, and those who carried crosses, and those who carried pots and pans, and cushions and books, and those who rang bells, and those who made a smoke, and those who sprinkled water, and those who bobbed their heads, and those who bowed their knees, the whole concern was very wonderful to look at, very amazing, very amusing, very childish. One wonders, when he sees it, whatever it is all about, and what kind of people those must be who are really made better by it. One marvels also what an idea pious Romanists must have of God if they imagine that He is pleased with such performances. Do you not wonder how the good Lord endures it? What must His glorious mind think of it all?

The glorious God cares nothing for pomp and show; but when you call upon Him in the day of trouble, and ask Him to deliver you, there is meaning in your groan of anguish. This is no empty form; there is heart in it, is there not? There is meaning in the appeal of sorrow, and therefore God prefers the prayer of a broken heart to the finest service that ever was performed by priests and choirs.

Why does God prefer realism to Ritualism? It is for this reason also that *there is something spiritual in the cry of a troubled heart ;* and "God is a Spirit: and they that worship him must worship him in spirit and in truth." Suppose I were to repeat to-night the finest creed for accuracy that was ever composed by learned and orthodox men; yet, if I had no faith in it, and you had none, what were the use of the repetition of the words? There is nothing spiritual in mere orthodox statement if we have no real belief therein: we might as well repeat the alphabet, and call it devotion. And if we were to burst forth to-night in the grandest hallelujah that ever pealed from mortal lips, and we did not mean it, there would be nothing spiritual in it, and it would be nothing to God. But when a poor soul gets away into its chamber, and bows its knee and cries, "God be merciful to me! God save me! God help me in this day of trouble!" there is spiritual life in such a cry, and therefore God approves it and answers it. Spiritual worship is that which He wants, and He will have it, or have nothing. "They that worship him *must* worship him in spirit and in truth." He has abolished the ceremonial law, destroyed the one altar at Jerusalem, burned the Temple, abolished the Aaronic priesthood, and ended for ever all ritualistic performance; for He seeketh only true worshippers, who worship Him in spirit and in truth.

Further, the Lord loves the cry of the broken heart because *it distinctly recognizes Himself as the living God,* in very deed sought after in prayer. From much of outward devotion God is absent. But how we mock God when we do not discern Him as present, and do not come nigh unto His very self! When the heart, the mind, the soul, breaks through itself to get to its God, then it is that God is glorified, but not by any bodily exercises in which He is forgotten. Oh, how real God is to a man who is perishing, and feels that only God can save him! He believes that God is, or else he would not make so piteous a prayer to Him. He said his prayers before, and little cared whether God heard or not; but he prays now, and God's hearing is his chief anxiety.

Besides, dear friends, God takes great delight in our crying to Him in the day of trouble because *there is sincerity in it.* I am afraid that in the hour of our mirth and the day of our prosperity many of our prayers and our thanksgivings are hypocrisy. Too many of us are like boys' tops, that cease to spin except they are whipped. Certainly we pray with a deep intensity when we get into great trouble. A man is very poor: he is out of a situation; he has worn his shoes out in trying to find work; he does not know where the next meal is coming from for his children; and if he prays now it is likely to be very sincere prayer, for he is in real earnest on account of real trouble. I have sometimes wished for some very gentlemanly Christian people, who seem to treat religion as if it were all kid gloves, that they could have just a little time of the "roughing" of it, and really come into actual difficulties. A life of ease breeds hosts of falsehoods and pretences, which would soon vanish in the presence of matter-of-fact trials.

Many a man has been converted to God in the bush of Australia by hunger, and weariness, and loneliness, who, when he was a wealthy man, surrounded by gay flatterers, never thought of God at all. Many a man on board ship on yon Atlantic has learned to pray in the cold chill of an iceberg, or in the horrors of the trough of the wave out of which the vessel could not rise. When the mast has gone by the board, and every timber has been strained, and the ship has seemed doomed, then have hearts begun to pray in sincerity; and God loves sincerity. When we mean it; when the soul melts in prayer; when it is "I must have it, or be lost"; when it is no sham, no vain performance, but a real heart-breaking, agonizing cry, then God accepts it. Hence He says, "Call upon me in the day of trouble." Such a cry is the kind of worship that He cares for, because there is sincerity in it, and this is acceptable with the God of truth.

Again, in the cry of the troubled one *there is humility*. We may go through a highly brilliant performance of religion, after the rites of some gaudy church; or we may go through our own rites, which are as simple as they can be; and we may be all the while saying to ourselves, "This is very nicely done." The preacher may be thinking, "Am I not preaching well?" The brother at the prayer-meeting may feel within himself, "How delightfully fluent I am!" Whenever there is that spirit in us, God cannot accept our worship. Worship is not acceptable if it be devoid of humility. Now, when in the day of trouble a man goes to God, and says, "Lord, help me! I cannot help myself, but do Thou interpose for me," there is humility in that confession and cry, and hence the Lord takes delight in them.

Once more, the Lord loves such pleadings because *there is a measure of faith in them*. When the man in trouble cries, "Lord, deliver me!" he is looking away from himself. You see, he is driven out of himself because of the famine that is in the land. He cannot find hope or help on earth, and therefore he looks towards heaven. God loves to discover even the shadow of faith in His unbelieving creature. When faith does, as it were, only cross over the field of the camera, so that across the photograph there is a dim trace of its having been there, God can spy it out, and He can and will accept prayer for the sake of that little faith. Oh, dear heart, where art thou? Art thou torn with anguish? Art thou sore distressed? Art thou lonely? Art thou cast away? Then cry to God. None else can help thee; now art thou shut up to Him. Blessed shutting up! Cry to Him, for He can help thee; and I tell thee, in that cry of thine there will be a pure and true worship, such as God desires, far more than the slaughter of ten thousand bullocks, or the pouring out of rivers of oil. It is true, assuredly, from Scripture, that the groan of a burdened spirit is among the sweetest sounds that are ever heard by the ear of the Most High. Plaintive cries are anthems with Him, to whom all mere arrangements of sound must be as child's-play.

See then, poor, weeping, and distracted ones, that it is not Ritualism, it is not the performance of pompous ceremonies, it is not bowing and scraping, it is not using sacred words; but it is crying to God in the hour of your trouble; which is the most acceptable sacrifice your spirit can bring before the throne of God.

II. Come we now to our second observation. May God impress it upon us all! In our text we have ADVERSITY TURNED TO ADVANTAGE. "Call upon me in the day of trouble: I will deliver thee."

H

We say it with all reverence, but God Himself cannot deliver a man who is not in trouble, and therefore it is some advantage to be in distress, because God can then deliver you. Even Jesus Christ, the Healer of men, cannot heal a man who is not sick; so that it turns to our advantage to be sick, in order that Christ may heal us. Thus, my hearer, your adversity may prove your advantage by offering occasion and opportunity for the display of divine grace. It is great wisdom to learn the art of making honey out of gall, and the text teaches us how to do that; it shows how trouble can become gain. When you are in adversity, then call upon God, and you shall experience a deliverance which will be a richer and sweeter experience for your soul than if you had never known trouble. Here is the art and science of making gains out of losses, and advantages out of adversities.

Now let me suppose that there is some person here in trouble. Perhaps another deserted Robinson Crusoe is among us. I am not idly supposing that a tried individual is here; he is so. Well now, when you pray—and oh! I wish you would pray now—do you not see what a plea you have? You have first a plea from *the time ;* "Call upon me in the day of trouble." You can plead, "Lord, this is a day of trouble! I am in great affliction, and my case is urgent at this hour." Then state what your trouble is— that sick wife, that dying child, that sinking business, that failing health, that situation which you have lost—that poverty which stares you in the face. Say unto the Lord of mercy, "My Lord, if ever a man was in a day of trouble, I am that man; and there-fore I take leave and license to pray to Thee now, because Thou hast said, 'Call upon me in the day of trouble.' This is the hour which Thou has appointed for appealing to Thee: this dark, this stormy day. If ever there was a man that had a right given him to pray by thy own word, I am that man, for I am in trouble, and therefore I will make use of the very time as a plea with Thee. Do, I beseech Thee, hear Thy servant's cry in this midnight hour."

Further, turn your adversity to advantage by pleading *the command.* You can go to the Lord now, at this precise instant, and say, "Lord, do hear me, for Thou hast commanded me to pray! I, though I am evil, would not tell a man to ask a thing of me, if I intended to deny him; I would not urge him to ask help, if I meant to refuse it." Do you not know brethren, that we often impute to the good Lord conduct which we should be ashamed of in ourselves? This must not be. If you said to a poor man, "You are in very sad circumstances; write to me to-morrow, and I will see to your affairs for you"; and if he did write to you, you would not treat his letter with contempt. You would be bound to consider his case. When you told him to write, you meant that you would help him if you could. And when God tells you to call upon Him, He does not mock you: He means that He will deal kindly with you. I do not know who you are. You may be Robinson Crusoe, for aught I know, but you may call on the Lord, for He bids you call; and, if you do call upon Him, you can put this argument into your prayer:

> " Lord, thou hast bid me seek thy face;
>   And shall I seek in vain?
>   And shall the ear of sovereign grace
>   Be deaf when I complain?"

So plead the time, and plead the trouble, and plead the command; and then plead with God *his own character*. Speak with Him reverently, but believingly, in this fashion, "Lord, it is Thou Thyself to Whom I appeal. Thou has said, 'Call upon me.' If my neighbour had bidden me do so, I might have feared that perhaps he would not hear me, but would change his mind; but Thou art too great and good to change. Lord, by Thy truth and by Thy faithfulness, by Thy immutability and by Thy love, I, a poor sinner, heart-broken and crushed, call upon Thee in the day of trouble! Oh, help Thou me, and help me soon; or else I die!" Surely you that are in trouble have many and mighty pleas. You are on firm ground with the angel of the covenant, and may bravely seize the blessing I do not feel to-night as if the text encouraged *me* one-half so much as it must encourage others of you, for I am not in trouble just now, and you are. I thank God I am full of joy and rest; but I am half inclined to see if I cannot patch up a little bit of trouble for myself: surely if I were in trouble, and sitting in those pews, I would open my mouth, and drink in this text, and pray like David, or Elias, or Daniel, in the power of this promise, "Call upon me in the day of trouble: I will deliver thee, and thou shalt glorify me."

O, you troubled ones, leap up at the sound of this word! Believe it. Let it go down into your souls. "The Lord looseth the prisoners." He has come to loose you. I can see my Master arrayed in His silken garments, His countenance is joyous as heaven, His face is bright as a morning without clouds, and in His hand He bears a silver key. "Whither away, my Master, with that silver key of thine?" "I go," saith he, "to open the door to the captive, and to loosen every one that is bound." Blessed Master, fulfil Thy errand; but pass not these prisoners of hope! We will not hinder Thee for a moment; but do not forget these mourners! Go up these galleries, and down these aisles, and set free the prisoners of Giant Despair, and make their hearts to sing

for joy because they have called upon Thee in the day of trouble,
and Thou has delivered them and they shall glorify Thee!

III. My third head is clearly in the text. Here we have FREE
GRACE LAID UNDER BONDS.

Nothing in heaven or earth can be freer than grace, but here
is grace putting itself under bonds of promise and convenant.
Listen. "Call upon me in the day of trouble: *I will deliver thee.*"
If a person has once said to you, "I will," you hold him; he has
placed himself at the command of his own declaration. If he is a
true man, and has plainly said, "I will," you have him in your
hand. He is not free after giving a promise as he was before it;
he has set himself a certain way, and he must keep to it. Is it not
so? I say so with the deepest reverence towards my Lord and
Master, He has bound Himself in the text with cords that He
cannot break. He must now hear and help those who call upon
Him in the day of trouble. He has solemnly promised, and He
will fully perform.

Notice that this text is *unconditional as to the persons.* It contains
the gist of that other promise—"Whosoever calleth upon the
name of the Lord shall be saved." The people who are specially
addressed in the text had mocked God; they had presented their
sacrifices without a true heart; but yet the Lord said to each of
them, "Call upon me in the day of trouble: I will deliver thee."
Hence I gather that He excludes none from the promise. Thou
atheist, thou blasphemer, thou unchaste and impure one, if
thou callest upon the Lord now, in this the day of thy trouble
He will deliver thee! Come and try Him. "If there be a God,"
sayest thou? But there is a God, say I; come, put Him to the test,
and see. He saith, "Call upon me in the day of trouble: I will
deliver thee." Will you not prove Him now? Come hither, ye bon-
daged ones, and see if He doth not free you! Come ye to Christ,
all ye that labour, and are heavy laden, and He will give you rest!
In temporals and in spirituals, but specially in spiritual things,
call upon Him in the day of trouble, and He will deliver you.

Moreover, notice that this "I will" *includes all needful power
which may be required for deliverance.* "Call upon me in the day of
trouble: I will deliver thee." "But how can this be?" cries one.
Ah! that I cannot tell you, and I do not feel bound to tell you:
it rests with the Lord to find suitable ways and means. God says,
"I will." Let Him do it in His own way. If He says, "I will,"
depend upon it He will keep His word. If it be needful to shake
heaven and earth, He will do it; for He cannot lack power, and
He certainly does not lack honesty; and an honest man will
keep his word at all costs, and so will a faithful God. Hear Him
say, "I will deliver thee," and ask no more questions. I do

not suppose that Daniel knew how God would deliver him out of the den of lions. I do not suppose that Joseph knew how he would be delivered out of the prison when his mistress had slandered his character so shamefully. I do not suppose that these ancient believers dreamed of the way of the Lord's deliverance; but they left themselves in God's hands. They rested upon God, and He delivered them in the best possible manner. He will do the like for you; only call upon Him, and then stand still, and see the salvation of God.

Notice, *the text does not say exactly when.* "I will deliver thee" is plain enough; but whether it shall be to-morrow, or next week, or next year, is not so clear. You are in a great hurry; but the Lord is not. Your trial may not yet have wrought all the good to you that it was sent to do, and therefore it must last longer. When the gold is cast into the fining-pot, it might cry to the goldsmith, "Let me out." "No," saith he, "you have not yet lost your dross. You must tarry in the fire till I have purified you." God may therefore subject us to many trials; and yet if He says, "I will deliver thee," depend upon it He will keep His word. The Lord's promise is like a good bill from a substantial firm. A bill may be dated for three months ahead; but anybody will discount it if it bears a trusted name. When you get God's "I will," you may always cash it by faith; and no discount need be taken from it, for it is current money of the merchant even when it is only "I will." God's promise for the future is good *bonâ fide* stuff for the present, if thou hast but faith to use it, "Call upon me in the day of trouble: I will deliver thee," is tantamount to deliverance already received. It means, "If I do not deliver thee now, I will deliver thee at a time that is better than now, when, if thou wert as wise as I am, thou wouldst prefer to be delivered rather than now."

But promptitude is implied, for else deliverance would not be wrought. "Ah!" says one, "I am in such a trouble that if I do not get deliverance soon I shall die." Rest assured that you shall not die. You shall be delivered, and therefore you shall be delivered before you quite die of despair. He will deliver you in the best possible time. The Lord is always punctual. You never were kept waiting by Him. You have kept Him waiting long enough; but He is prompt to the instant. He never keeps His servants waiting one single tick of the clock beyond His own appointed, fitting, wise, and proper moment. "I will deliver thee," implies that His delays will not be too protracted, less the spirit of man should fail because of hope deferred. The Lord rideth on the wings of the wind when He comes to the rescue of those who seek Him. Wherefore, be of good courage!

Oh, this is a blessed text! and yet what can I do with it? I cannot carry it home to those of you who want it most. Spirit of the living God, come thou, and apply these rich consolations to those hearts which are bleeding and ready to die!

Do notice this text once again. Let me repeat it, putting the emphasis in a different way: "Call upon *me* in the day of trouble, and *I* will deliver *thee*." Pick up the threads of those two words. "*I* will deliver thee; men would not; angels could not; but I will." God Himself will set about the rescue of the man that calls upon Him. It is yours to call: and it is God's to answer. Poor trembler, you begin to try to answer your own prayers! Why did you pray to God then? When you have prayed, leave it to God to fulfil His own promise. He says, "Do thou call upon me, and *I* will deliver thee."

Now take up that other word: "I will deliver *thee*." I know what you are thinking, Mr. John. You murmur, "God will deliver everybody, I believe, but *not me*." But the text saith, "I will deliver *thee*." It is the man that calls that shall get the answer. Mary, where art thou? If thou callest upon God He will answer *thee*. He will give *thee* the blessing even to thy own heart and spirit, in thy own personal experience. "Call upon me," says He, "in the day of trouble: I will deliver *thee*." Oh, for grace to take that personal pronoun home to one's soul, and to make sure of it as though you could see it with your own eyes!

The apostle tells us, "Through faith we understand that the worlds were framed by the Word of God." Assuredly I know that the worlds were made by God. I am sure of it; and yet I did not see Him making them. I did not see Him when the light came because He said, "Let there be light." I did not see Him divide the light from the darkness, and the waters that are beneath the firmament from the waters that are above the firmament, but I am quite sure that He did all this. All the evolution gentlemen in the world cannot shake my conviction that creation was wrought by God, though I was not there to see Him make even a bird, or a flower. Why should I not have just the same kind of faith to-night about God's answer to my prayer if I am in trouble? If I cannot see how He will deliver me, why should I wish to see? He created the world well enough without my knowing how He was to do it, and He will deliver me without my having a finger in it. It is no business of mine to see how He works. My business is to trust in my God, and glorify Him by believing that what He has promised He is able to perform.

IV. Thus we have had three sweet things to remember; and we close with a fourth, which is this: here are GOD AND THE PRAYING MAN TAKING SHARES.

That is an odd word to close with, but I want you to notice it. Here are the shares. First, here is your share: "Call upon me in the day of trouble." Secondly, here is God's share: "I will deliver thee." Again, you take a share—for you shall be delivered. And then again it is the Lord's turn—"Thou shalt glorify me." Here is a compact, a covenant that God enters into with you who pray to Him, and whom He helps. He says, "You shall have the deliverance, but I must have the glory. You shall pray; I will bless; and then you shall honour My holy name. Here is a delightful partnership: we obtain that which we so greatly need, and all that God getteth is the glory which is due unto His name.

Poor troubled heart! I am sure you do not demur to these terms. "Sinners," saith the Lord, "I will give you pardon, but you must give Me the honour of it." Our only answer is, "Ay, Lord, that we will, for ever and ever."

> "Who is a pardoning God like thee?
> Or who has grace so rich and free?"

"Come, souls," says He, "I will justify you, but I must have the glory of it." And our answer is, "Where is boasting, then? It is excluded. By the law of works? Nay, but by the law of faith." God must have the glory if we are justified by Christ.

"Come," says He, "I will put you into My family, but My grace must have the glory of it;" and we say, "Ay, that it shall, good Lord! Behold, what manner of love the Father hath bestowed upon us that we should be called the sons of God."

"Now," says He, "I will sanctify you, and make you holy, but I must have the glory of it;" and our answer is, "Yes, we will sing for ever—'We have washed our robes, and made them white in the blood of the Lamb. Therefore will we serve Him day and night in His temple, giving Him all praise.'"

"I will take you home to heaven," says God: "I will deliver you from sin and death and hell; but I must have the glory of it." "Truly," say we, "Thou shalt be magnified. For ever and for ever we will sing, 'Blessing, and honour, and glory, and power be unto Him that sitteth upon the throne, and unto the Lamb, for ever and ever.'"

Stop, you thief, there! What are you at? Running away with a portion of God's glory? What a villain he must be! Here is a man that was lately a drunkard, and God has loved him and made him sober, and he is wonderfully proud because he is sober. What folly! Have done, sir! Have done! Give God the glory of your deliverance from the degrading vice, or else you are still degraded by ingratitude. Here is another man. He used to swear once; but he has been praying now; he even delivered a sermon the other night, or at least an open-air address. He has been as proud about this as any peacock. O bird of pride, when you look at your fine feathers, remember your black feet, and your hideous voice! O reclaimed sinner, remember your former character, and be ashamed! Give God the glory if you have ceased to be profane. Give God the glory for every part of your salvation.

"Call upon me in the day of trouble. I will deliver thee"— that is your part. But "Thou shalt glorify me"—that is God's part. He must have all the honour from first to last.

Go out henceforth, you saved ones, and tell out what the Lord has done for you. An aged woman once said that if the Lord Jesus Christ really did save her, He should never hear the last of it. Join with her in that resolve. Truly my soul vows that my delivering Lord shall never hear the last of my salvation.

> " I'll praise him in life, and praise him in death,
> And praise him as long as he lendeth me breath;
> And say when the death-dew lies cold on my brow,
> ' If ever I loved thee, my Jesus, 'tis now.' "

Come, poor soul, you that came in here to-night in the deepest of trouble, God means to glorify Himself by you! The day shall yet come when you shall comfort other mourners by the rehearsal of your happy experience. The day may yet come when you that were a castaway shall preach the gospel to castaways. The day shall yet come, poor fallen woman, when you shall lead other sinners to the Saviour's feet, where now you stand weeping! Thou abandoned of the devil, whom even Satan is tired of, whom the world rejects because thou art worn out and stale—the day shall yet come when, renewed in heart, and washed in the blood of the Lamb, thou shalt shine like a star in the firmament, to the praise of the glory of His grace who hath made thee to be accepted in the Beloved! O desponding sinner, come to Jesus! Do call upon Him, I entreat you! Be persuaded to call upon your God and Father. If you can do no more than groan, groan unto God. Drop a tear, heave a sigh, and let your heart say to the Lord, "O God, deliver me, for Christ's sake! Save me from my sin and the consequences of it." As surely as you thus pray, He will hear you, and say, "Thy sins be forgiven thee. Go in peace." So may it be. Amen.

A FREE GRACE PROMISE

A Sermon

Text.—"And it shall come to pass, that whosoever shall call on the name of the Lord shall be delivered."—Joel ii. 32.

VENGEANCE was in full career. The armies of divine justice had been called forth for war: "They shall run like mighty men; they shall climb the wall like men of war." They had invaded and devastated the land, and turned the land from being like the garden of Eden into a desolate wilderness. All faces gathered blackness: the people were "much pained." The sun itself was dim, the moon was dark, and the stars withdrew themselves: the earth quaked, and the heavens trembled. At such a dreadful time, when we might least have expected it, between the peals of thunder and the flashes of lightning, was heard this gentle word, "It shall come to pass, that whosoever shall call on the name of the Lord shall be delivered."

Let us carefully read the passage: "And I will show wonders in the heavens and in the earth, blood, and fire, and pillars of smoke. The sun shall be turned into darkness, and the moon into blood, before the great and the terrible day of the Lord come. And it shall come to pass, that whosoever shall call on the name of the Lord shall be delivered." In the worst times that can ever happen, there is still salvation for men. When day turns to night, and life becomes death, and the staff of life is broken, and the hope of man has fled, there still remains in God, in the person of His dear Son, deliverance to all those who will call upon the name of the Lord. We do not know what is to happen: reading the roll of the future, we prophesy dark things; but still this light shall always shine between the rifts of the cloud-wrack: "Whosoever shall call on the name of the Lord shall be delivered."

This passage was selected by the apostle at Pentecost to be set in its place as a sort of morning star of gospel times. When the Spirit was poured out upon the servants and the handmaids, and sons and daughters began to prophesy, it was clear that the wondrous time had come, which had been foretold so long before. Then Peter, as he preached his memorable sermon, told the people, "Whosoever shall call on the name of the Lord shall be saved"; thus giving a fuller and yet more evangelical meaning to the word "delivered." "Whosoever shall call on the name of the Lord shall be delivered" from sin, death and hell—shall, in fact, be so delivered as to be, in divine language, "saved"—saved from

117

guilt, the penalty, the power of sin, saved from the wrath to come. These gospel times are still the happy days in which "whosoever shall call on the name of the Lord shall be saved." In the Year of Grace we have reached a day and an hour in which "whosoever shall call on the name of the Lord shall be saved." To you at this moment is this salvation sent. The dispensation of immediate acceptance proclaimed at Pentecost has never ceased: its fulness of blessing has grown rather than diminished. The sacred promise stands in all its certainty, fulness, and freeness: it has lost none of all its breadth and length: "Whosoever shall call on the name of the Lord shall be saved."

I have nothing to do to-night but to tell you over again the old, old story of infinite mercy come to meet infinite sin—of free grace come to lead free will into a better line of things—of God Himself appearing to undo man's ruin wrought by man, and to lift him up by a great deliverance. May the Holy Spirit graciously aid me while I shall talk to you very simply, thus:—

I. First, THERE IS SOMETHING ALWAYS WANTED. That something is deliverance, or "salvation." *It is always wanted*. It is the requisite of man, wherever man is found. As long as there are men on the face of the earth, there will always be a need of salvation. If we could go through London, into its dens and slums, we should think very differently of human need from what we do when we simply come from our own quiet domestic circle, and step into our pew and hear a sermon. The world is still sick and dying. The world is still corrupting and rotting. The world is a ship in which the water is rising fast, and the vessel is going down into the deep of destruction. God's salvation is wanted as much to-day as when the spirit preached it in Noah's day to the spirits in prison. God must step in, and bring deliverance, or there remains no hope.

Some want deliverance from present trouble. If you are in this need to-night through very sore distress, I invite you to take my text as your guide, and believe that "whosoever shall call on the name of the Lord shall be delivered." Depend upon it, in any form of distress, physical, mental, or whatever it may be, prayer is wonderfully available. "Call upon me," says God, "in the day of trouble: I will deliver thee, and thou shalt glorify me."

This is true whenever you come into a position of deep personal distress, even though it should not be of a physical kind. When you do not know how to act, but are bewildered and at your wits' end, when wave of trouble has followed wave of trouble till you are like the sailor in the storm who reels to and fro, and staggers like a drunken man; if now you cannot help yourself, because your spirit sinks and your mind fails, call upon God, call upon God, call upon God! Lost child in the wood, with the night fog

thickening about you, ready to lie down and die, call upon your
Father! Call upon God, thou distracted one; for "Whosoever
shall call on the name of the Lord shall be delivered."

In the last great day when all secrets are known, it will seem
ridiculous that ever persons took to writing tales and romances;
for the real stories of what God has done for those who cry to
Him are infinitely more surprising. If men and women could
but tell in simple, natural language how God has come to their
rescue in the hour of imminent distress, they would set the harps
of heaven a-ringing with new melodies, and the heart of saints
on earth a-glowing with new love to God for His wonderful kindness to the children of men. Oh that men would praise the Lord
for His goodness! Oh that we could abundantly utter the memory
of His great goodness to ourselves in the night of our weeping!

The text holds good concerning deliverance from future troubles. What is
to happen in the amazing future we do not know. Whatever is to
happen according to the Word of God—if the sun shall be turned
into darkness and the moon into blood—if God shall show great
wonders in the heavens, and in the earth, blood and fire, and
pillars of smoke, yet remember that though you will then assuredly
want deliverance, deliverance will still be near at hand. The
text seems put in a startling connection in order to advise us
that when the worst and most terrible convulsions shall occur,
"Whosoever shall call on the name of the Lord shall be saved."
The star Wormwood may fall, but we shall be saved if we call upon
the name of the Lord. Plagues may be poured out, trumpets
may sound, and judgments may follow one another as quickly
as the plagues of Egypt, but "Whosoever shall call on the name
of the Lord shall be saved." When the need of deliverance shall
apparently increase, the abundance of salvation shall increase
with it. Fear not the direst of all wars, the bitterest of all famines,
the deadliest of all plagues; for still, if we call upon the Lord, He
is pledged to deliver us. This word of promise meets the most
terrible of possibilities with a sure salvation.

Yes, and when you come to die, when to you the sun has turned
into darkness, and the moon into blood, *this text ensures deliverance
in the last dread hour.* Call upon the name of the Lord, and you shall
be saved. Amid the pains of death, and the gloom of departure,
you shall enjoy a glorious visitation, which shall turn darkness
into light, and sorrow into joy. When you wake up amid the
realities of the eternal future there will be nothing for you to dread
in resurrection, or in judgment, or in the yawning mouth of hell.
If you have called upon the name of the Lord, you shall still be
delivered. Though the unpardoned are thrust down to the depth
of woe, and the righteous scarcely are saved, yet you who have

called upon the name of the Lord must be delivered. Stands the promise firm, whatever may be hidden in the great roll of the future; God cannot deny Himself, He will deliver those who call upon His name.

What is wanted, then, is salvation; and I do think, beloved brethren, that you and I who preach the Word, and long to save souls, must very often go over this grand old truth about salvation to the guilty, deliverance to all who call upon the name of the Lord. Sometimes we talk to friends about the higher life, about attaining to very high degrees of sanctity; and all this is very proper and very good; but still the great fundamental truth is, "Whosoever shall call on the name of the Lord shall be saved." We urge our friends to be sound in doctrine, and to know what they do know, and to understand the revealed will of God; and very proper is this also; but still, first and foremost, this is the elementary, all-important truth—"Whosoever shall call on the name of the Lord shall be saved." To this old foundation truth we come back for comfort.

I sometimes rejoice in God, and joy in the God of my salvation, and spread my wings and mount up into communion with the heavenlies; but still there are other seasons when I hide my head in darkness, and then I am very glad of such a broad, gracious promise as this, "Whosoever shall call on the name of the Lord shall be saved." I find that my sweetest, happiest, safest state, is just as a poor, guilty, helpless sinner, to call upon the name of the Lord, and take mercy at His hands as one who deserves nothing but His wrath, while I dare hang the weight of my soul on such a sure promise as this, "Whosoever shall call on the name of the Lord shall be saved." Get where you may, however high your experience; be what you may, however great your usefulness, you will always want to come back to the same ground upon which the poorest and weakest of hearts must stand, and claim to be saved by almighty grace, through simply calling upon the name of the Lord.

Thus have I said enough upon what is always wanted—this deliverance, this salvation.

II. Now, secondly, let us attentively observe THE WAY IN WHICH THIS DELIVERANCE IS TO BE HAD. Help us, blessed Spirit, in this our meditation. It is to be had, according to the text, by calling upon the name of the Lord.

Is not the most obvious sense of this language, *prayer*? Are we not brought to the Lord by a prayer which trusts in God—by a prayer which asks God to give the deliverance that is needed, and expects to have it from the Lord, as a gift of grace? It amounts to much the same thing as that other word "Believe and live"; for how shall they call on Him of Whom they have not heard? And if they have heard, yet vain is their calling if they have not believed as well as heard. But to "call on the name of the Lord," is briefly to pray a believing prayer; to cry to God for His help, and to leave yourself in His hands. This is very simple, is it not? There is no cumbersome machinery here, nothing complex and mysterious. No priestly help is wanted, except the help of that great High Priest, who intercedes for us within the vell. A poor, broken heart pours its distress into the ear of God, and calls upon Him to fulfil His promise of help in the time of need—that is all. Thank God, nothing more is mentioned in our text. The promise is—"Whosoever shall call on the name of the Lord shall be saved."

The text, however, contains within it a measure of specific instruction: *the prayer must be to the true God.* "Whosoever shall call on the name of Jehovah shall be saved." There is something distinctive here; for one would call on Baal, another would call on Ashtaroth, and a fourth on Moloch; but these would not be saved. The promise is special: "Whosoever shall call on the name of Jehovah shall be saved." You know that triune name, "Father, Son and Holy Ghost"—call upon it. You know how the name of Jehovah is set forth most conspicuously in the person of the Lord Jesus—call upon Him. Call upon the true God. Call upon no idol, call on no Virgin Mary, no saint, dead or living. Call on no image. Call on no impression of your mind! Call upon the living God—call upon Him who reveals Himself in the Bible—call upon Him who manifests Himself in the person of His dear Son; for whosoever shall call upon this God shall be saved. You may call upon the idols, but these will not hear you: "Ears have they, but they hear not. Eyes have they, but they see not." You may not call upon men, for they are all sinners like yourselves. Priests cannot help their most zealous admirers; but, "Whosoever shall call on the name of Jehovah shall be saved." Mind, then, it is not the mere repetition of a prayer as a sort of charm, or a piece of religious witchcraft, but you must make a direct address to God, an appeal to the Most High to help you in your time of need. In presenting true prayer to the true God you shall be delivered.

Moreover, *the prayer should be intelligently presented.* We read, "Whosoever shall call on *the name* of the Lord." Now, by the word "name" we understand the person, the character of the Lord. The more, then, you know about the Lord, and the better you know His name, the more intelligently will you call upon that name. If you know His power, you will call upon that power to help you. If you know His mercy, you will call upon Him in

His grace to save you. If you know His wisdom, you feel that He knows your difficulties, and can help you through them. If you understand His immutability, you will call upon Him, as the same God who has saved other sinners, to come and save *you*. It will be well, therefore, for you to study the Scriptures much, and to pray the Lord to manifest Himself to you that you may know Him; since, in proportion to your acquaintance with Him, will you with greater confidence be able to call upon His name. But, little as you may know, call on Him according to the little you do know. Cast yourself upon Him, whether your trouble to-night be external or internal; but especially if it be internal, if it be the trouble of sin, if it be the burden of guilt, if it be a load of horror and fear because of wrath to come, call upon the name of the Lord, for you shall be delivered. There stands His promise. It is not, "He may be delivered," but he "*shall* be." Note well the everlasting "shall" of God—irrevocable, unalterable, unquestionable, irresistible. His promise stands eternally the same. Hath He said, and shall He not do it? "Whosoever shall call on the name of the Lord shall be saved."

This way of salvation, by calling upon the name of the Lord, *glorifies God*. He asks nothing of you but that you ask everything of Him. You are the beggar, and He is the benefactor. You are in the trouble, and He is the Deliverer. All you have to do is to trust Him, and beg of Him. This is easy enough. This puts the matter into the hands of the Lord, and takes it out of your hands. Do you not like the plan? Put it in practice immediately! It will prove itself gloriously effectual.

Dear friends, I speak to some whom I know to be now present, who are under severe trial. You dare not look up. You seem to be given up; at any rate you have given yourself up; and yet I pray you, call upon the name of the Lord. You cannot perish praying; no one has ever done so. If you could perish praying, you would be a new wonder in the universe. A praying soul in hell is an utter impossibility. A man calling on God and rejected of God!—the supposition is not to be endured. "Whosoever shall call on the name of the Lord shall be saved." God Himself must lie, He must quit His nature, forfeit His claim to mercy, destroy His character of love, if He were to let a poor sinner call upon His name, and yet refuse to hear him. There will come a day, but that is not now—there will come a day in the next state when He will say, "I called, but ye refused"; but it is not so now. While there is life there is hope. "To-day if ye will hear His voice, harden not your heart," but call upon God at once; for this warrant of grace runneth through all the regions of mortality, "Whosoever shall call on the name of the Lord shall be saved."

I recollect a time when, if I had heard a sermon on this subject, putting it plainly to me, I should have leaped into comfort and light in a single moment. Is it not such a time with you? I thought, I must *do* something, I must *be* something, I must in some way prepare myself for the mercy of God. I did not know that a calling upon God, a trusting myself in His hand, an invocation of His sacred name, would bring me to Christ, the Saviour. But so it stands, and happy, indeed, was I when I found it out. Heaven is given away. Salvation may be had for the asking. I hope that many a captive heart here will at once leap to loose his chains, and cry, "It is even so. If God has said it, it must be true. There it is in His own Word. I have called upon Him, and I must be delivered."

III. Now I come to notice, in the third place, THE PEOPLE TO WHOM THIS PROMISE AND THIS DELIVERANCE WILL BE GIVEN. "Whosoever shall call upon the name of the Lord shall be delivered."

According to the connection, *the people had been greatly afflicted*—afflicted beyond all precedent, afflicted to the very brink of despair; but the Lord said, "Whosoever shall call on the name of the Lord shall be saved." Go down to the hospital. You may select, if you please, the hospital which deals with the effects of vice. In that house of misery you may stand at each bed and say, "Whosoever shall call on the name of the Lord shall be saved." You may then hasten to the jail. You may stop at every door of every cell, yes, even at the grating of the condemned cell, if there lie men and women there given up to death, and you may with safety say to each one, "Whosoever shall call on the name of the Lord shall be delivered."

I know what the Pharisees will say—"If you preach this, men will go on in sin." It has always been so, that the great mercy of God has been turned by some into a reason for continuing in sin; but God (and this is the wonder of it) has never restricted His mercy because of that. It must have been a terrible provocation of Almighty grace when men have perverted His mercy into an excuse for sin, but the Lord has never even taken the edges off from His mercy because men have misused it: He has still made it stand out bright and clear: "Whosoever shall call upon the name of the Lord shall be saved." Still He cries, "Turn and live." "Let the wicked forsake his way, and the unrighteous man his thoughts: and let him return unto the Lord, and He will have mercy upon him; and to our God, for He will abundantly pardon." Undimmed is that brave sun that shineth on the foulest dunghills of vice. Trust Christ, and live. Call upon the name of the Lord, and you shall be pardoned;

yea, you shall be rescued from the bondage of your sin, and be made a new creature, a child of God, a member of the family of His grace. The most afflicted, and the most afflicted by sin, are met with by this gracious promise, "Whosoever shall call on the name of the Lord shall be saved."

Yes, but there were some, according to Joel, *who had the Spirit of God poured out upon them.* What about them? Were they saved by that? Oh no! Those who had the Spirit of God so that they dreamed dreams and saw visions, yet had to come to the palace of mercy by this same gate of believing prayer—"Whosoever shall call on the name of the Lord shall be saved." Ah, poor souls! you say to yourselves, "if we were deacons of churches, if we were pastors, oh, then we should be saved!" You do not know anything about it: church officers are no more saved by their office than you are by being without office. We owe nothing to our official position in this matter of salvation: in fact, we may owe our damnation to our official standing unless we look well to our ways. We have no preference over you plain folks. I do assure you, I am quite happy to take your hand, whoever you may be, and come to Christ on the same footing as yourself.

> " Nothing in my hand I bring,
> Simply to thy cross I cling."

Often, when I have been cheering up a poor sinner, and urging him to believe in Christ, I have thought, "Well, if he will not drink this cup of comfort, I will even drink it up myself." I assure you, I need it as much as those to whom I carry it. I have been as big a sinner as any of you, and therefore I take the promise to myself. The divine cordial shall not be lost: I will accept it. I came to Jesus as I was, weary, and worn, and faint, and sick, and full of sin, and I trusted Him on my own account, and found peace—peace on the same ground as my text sets before all of you. If I drink of this consolation, you may drink it too. The miracle of this cup is that fifty may drink, and yet it is just as full as ever. There is no restriction in the word "Whosoever." You maidens that have the Spirit of God upon you, and you old men that dream, it is neither the Spirit of God nor the dreaming that will save you; but your calling on the sacred name. It is, "whosoever shall call on the name of the Lord shall be saved."

Also, there were *some upon whom the Spirit of God did not fall.* They did not speak with tongues, nor prophesy the future, nor work miracles, but though they did none of these marvels, yet it stood true to them—"Whosoever shall call on the name of the

Lord shall be saved." What though no supernatural gift was bestowed, though they saw no vision and could not speak with tongues, they called upon the name of the Lord, and they were saved. There is the same way of salvation for the little as well as for the great, for the poorest and most obscure as well as for those that are strong in faith, and lead the hosts of God to the battle.

"Ah!" says another, "but I am worse than that. I have *no good feelings*. I would give all that I have to own a broken heart. I wish I could even feel despair, but I am hard as a stone." I have been told that sorrowful story many times, and it almost always happens that those who most mourn their want of feeling are those who feel most acutely. Their hearts are like hell-hardened steel, so they say; but it is not true. But if it were true, "Whosoever shall call on the name of the Lord shall be saved." Do you think that the Lord wants you to give yourself a new heart first, and that then He will save you? My dear soul, you are saved when you have a new heart, and you do not want Him to save you then, since you are saved. "Oh, but I must get good feelings!" Must you? Where are you going for them? Are you to rake the dunghill of your depraved nature to find good feelings there? Come without any good feeling. Come just as you are. Come, you that are like a frozen iceberg, that have nothing about you whatever, but that which chills and repels; come and call upon the name of the Lord, and you shall be saved. "Wonders of grace to God belong." It is not a small gospel that He has sent us to preach to small sinners, but ours is a great gospel for great sinners. "Whosoever shall call on the name of the Lord shall be saved."

"Ah, well!" says one, "I cannot think it is meant for me, for *I am nobody*." Nobody, are you there? I have a great love for nobodies. I am worried with somebodies, and the worst somebody in the world is my own somebody. How I wish I could always turn my own somebody out, and keep company with none but nobodies! Then I should make Jesus everybody. Nobody, where are you? You are the very person that I am sent to look after. If there is nothing of you, there shall be all the more of Christ. If you are not only empty, but cracked and broken; if you are done for, destroyed, ruined, utterly crushed and broken, to you is this word of salvation sent:—"Whosoever shall call on the name of the Lord shall be saved."

I have set the gate wide open. If it were the wrong track, all the sheep would go through; but as it is the right road, I may set the gate open as long as I will, but yet the sheep will shun it, unless thou, Great Shepherd, shall go around the field to-night, and lead them in. Take up in Thine own arms some sheep that Thou hast purchased long ago with Thy dear heart's blood-—

I

take him upon Thy gracious shoulders, rejoicing as Thou doest it, and place him within the field where the good pasture grows.

IV. I want you to dwell for a minute upon THE BLESSING ITSELF. "Whosoever shall call on the name of the Lord *shall be delivered*." I need not say much about it because I have already expounded it. It is a very good rule, when *a man* makes you a promise, to understand it in the narrowest sense. It is fair to him that you should do so. Let *him* interpret it liberally, if *he* pleases; but he is actually bound to give you no more than the bare terms of his promise will imply. Now, it is a rule which all God's people may well practise, always to understand *God's* promises in the largest possible sense. If the words will bear a bigger construction than at the first sight they naturally suggest to you, you may put the larger construction upon them. "He is able to do exceeding abundantly above all that we ask or even think." God never draws a line in His promise, that He may go barely up to it; but it is with the great God as it was with His dear Son, who, though He was sent to the lost sheep of the house of Israel, yet spent the greater part of His time in Galilee, which was called, "Galilee of the Gentiles"; and went to the very verge of Canaan to find out a Canaanitish woman, that He might give her a blessing. Thou mayest put the biggest and most liberal sense, then, on such a text as this, for Peter did so. The New Testament is wont to give a broader sense to Old Testament words; and it does so most rightly, for God loves us to treat His words with the breadth of faith.

Come, then, if you are the subject of the judgments of God; if you believe that God's hand has visited you on account of sin, call upon Him, and He will deliver you both *from the judgment*, *and from the guilt* that brought the judgment—from the sin, and from that which follows the sin. He will help you to escape. Try Him now, I pray you.

And if your case should be different: if you are a child of God and you are in trouble, and that trouble eats into your spirit, and causes you daily wear of spirit and tear of heart—call upon the Lord. He can take away from you *the fret and the trouble too*. "Whosoever shall call on the name of the Lord shall be delivered." You may have to bear the trouble, but it shall be so transformed as to be rather a blessing than an evil, and you shall fall in love with your cross, since the nature of it has been changed.

If sin be the great cause of your present trouble, and that *sin has brought you into bondage* to evil habits, if you have been a drunkard and do not know how to learn sobriety, if you have been unchaste and have become entangled in vicious connections; call upon God, and He can break you away from the sin, and set you free from all its entanglements. He can cut you loose to-night with the great sword of His grace, and make you a free man. I tell you that, though you should be like a poor sheep between the jaws of a lion, ready to be devoured immediately by the monster, God can come and pluck you out from between the lion's jaws. The prey shall be taken from the mighty, and the lawful captive shall be delivered. Only call upon the name of the Lord! Call upon the name of the Lord, and you shall be delivered.

V. In conclusion, I must remind you of one mournful thought. Let me warn you of THE SADLY COMMON NEGLECT OF THIS BLESSING. You would think that everybody would call upon the name of the Lord; but read the text, "For in mount Zion and in Jerusalem shall be deliverance, as the Lord hath said." It shall be there as the Lord hath said. Will they not have it then? Notice! "And in the remnant whom the Lord shall call." It seems to shrivel me up altogether, that word "remnant." What! Will they not come? Are they madmen? Will they not come? No, only a remnant; and even that remnant will not call upon the name of the Lord until first God calls them by His grace. This is almost as great a wonder as the love which so graciously invites them. Could even devils behave worse? If they were invited to call upon God, and be saved, would they refuse?

Unhappy business! The way is plain, but "few there be that find it." After all the preaching, and all the invitation, and the illimitable breadth of the promise, yet all that are saved are contained "in the remnant whom the Lord shall call." Is not our text a generous invitation; the setting open of the door, yea, the lifting of the door from off its hinges, that it never might be shut? And yet "broad is the gate, and wide is the way that leadeth to destruction, and many there be that go in thereat." There they come, streams of them, hurrying impatiently, rushing down to death and hell—yes, eagerly panting, hurrying, dashing against one another to descend to that awful gulf from which there is no return! No missionaries are wanted, no ministers are needed to plead with men to go to hell. No books of persuasion are wanted to urge them to rush onward to eternal ruin.

Never spake the Master a word which observation more clearly proves than when He said, "Ye will not come to me, that ye might have life." You will attend your chapels, but you will not call on the Lord. Jesus cries, "Ye search the scriptures; for in them ye think ye have eternal life, and they are they which testify of me; but ye will not come to me, that ye might have life." You will do anything rather than come to Jesus. You stop short of calling upon Him. O my dear hearers, do not let it be so with you! Many of you are saved; I beseech you intercede for those who are not saved. Oh, that the unconverted among you may be moved to pray. Before you leave this place, breathe an earnest prayer to God, saying, "God be merciful to me a sinner. Lord I need to be saved. Save me. I call upon Thy name." Join with me in prayer at this moment, I entreat you. Join with me while I put words into your mouths, and speak them on your behalf—"Lord, I am guilty. I deserve Thy wrath. Lord I cannot save myself. Lord, I would have a new heart and a right spirit, but what can I do? Lord, I can do nothing, come and work in me to will and to do of Thy good pleasure.

> "I'll praise him in life, and praise him in death,
> And praise him as long as he lendeth me breath;
> And say when the death-dew lies cold on my brow,
> ' If ever I loved thee, my Jesus, 'tis now.'"

But I now do from my very soul call upon Thy name. Trembling, yet believing, I cast myself wholly upon thee, O Lord. I trust the blood and righteousness of Thy dear Son; I trust Thy mercy, and Thy love, and Thy power, as they are revealed in Him. I dare to lay hold upon this word of Thine, that whosoever shall call on the name of the Lord shall be saved. Lord, save me to-night, for Jesus' sake. Amen."

PLEADING, NOT CONTRADICTION

A Sermon

Text.—"She said, Truth, Lord: yet."—Matthew xv. 27.

Did you notice, in the reading of this narrative of the Syro-Phœnician woman, the two facts mentioned in the twenty-first and twenty-second verses? "Then Jesus went thence, and departed into the coasts of Tyre and Sidon. And, behold, a woman of Canaan came out of the same coasts." See, Jesus goes towards the coast of Sidon on the land side, and the woman of Canaan comes from the sea-shore to meet Him; and so they come to the same town. May we find that case repeated this morning in this Tabernacle! May our Lord Jesus come into this congregation with power to cast out the devil; and may some one—nay, may many—have come to this place on purpose to seek grace at His hands! Blessed shall be this day's meeting! See how the grace of God arranges things. Jesus and the seeker have a common attraction. He comes, and she comes. It would have been of no use her coming from the sea-coast of Tyre and Sidon if the Lord Jesus had not also come down to the Israelite border of Phœnicia to meet her. His coming makes her coming a success. What a happy circumstance when Christ meets the sinner, and the sinner meets his Lord!

Our Lord Jesus, as the Good Shepherd, came that way, drawn by the instincts of His heart: He was seeking after lost ones, and He seemed to feel that there was one to be found on the borders of Tyre and Sidon, and, therefore, He must go that way to find that one. It does not appear that He preached, or did anything special upon the road; He left the ninety and nine by the sea of Galilee to seek that one lost sheep by the Mediterranean shore. When He had dealt with her He went back again to His old haunts in Galilee.

Our Lord was drawn towards this woman, but she, also, was driven towards Him. What made her seek Him? Strange to say, a devil had a hand in it; but not so as to give the devil any of the praise. The truth was that a gracious God used the devil Himself to drive this woman to Jesus: for her daughter was "grievously vexed with a devil," and she could not bear to stay at home and see her child in such misery. Oh, how often does a great sorrow drive men and women to Christ, even as a fierce wind compels the mariner to hasten to the harbour! I have known a domestic affliction, a daughter sore vexed, influence the heart of a mother to seek the Saviour; and, doubtless, many a father, broken in spirit by the likelihood of losing a darling child, has turned his face towards the Lord Jesus in his distress. Ah, my Lord! Thou hast many ways of bringing Thy wandering sheep back; and among the rest Thou dost even send the black dog of sorrow and of sickness after them. This dog comes into the house, and his howlings are so dreadful that the poor lost sheep flies to the Shepherd for shelter. God make it so this morning with any of you who have a great trouble at home! May your boy's sickness work your health! Yes, may your girl's death be the means of the father's spiritual life! Oh, that your soul and Jesus may meet this day! Your Saviour drawn by love, and your poor heart driven by anguish—may you thus be brought to a gracious meeting-place!

Now, you would suppose that as the two were seeking each other, the happy meeting and the gracious blessing would be very easily brought about; but we have an old proverb, that "the course of true love never does run smooth"; and for certain, the course of true faith is seldom without trials. Here was genuine love in the heart of Christ towards this woman, and genuine faith in her heart towards Christ; but difficulties sprang up which we should never have looked for. It is for the good of us all that they occurred, but we could not have anticipated them. Perhaps there were more difficulties in the way of this woman than of anybody else that ever came to Jesus in the days of His flesh. I never saw the Saviour before in such a mood as when He spake to this woman of great faith. Did you ever read of His speaking such rough words? Did such a hard sentence, at any other time, ever fall from His lips as, "It is not meet to take the children's bread, and to cast it to dogs"? Ah! He knew her well, and He knew that she could stand the trial, and would be greatly benefited by it, and that He would be glorified by her faith throughout all future ages: therefore with good reason He put her through the athletic exercises which train a vigorous faith. Doubtless, for our sakes, He drew her through a test to which He would never have exposed her had she been a weakling unable to sustain it. She was trained and developed by His rebuffs. While His wisdom tried her, His grace sustained her.

Now, see how He began. The Saviour was come to the town, wherever it was; but He was not there in public; on the contrary, He sought seclusion. Mark tells us, in his seventh chapter, at the twenty-fourth verse, "From thence he arose, and went into the borders of Tyre and Sidon, and entered into an house, and would have no man know it: but he could not be hid. For a certain woman, whose young daughter had an unclean spirit, heard of him, and came and fell at his feet."

Why is He hiding from her? He does not usually avoid the quest of the seeking soul. "Where is He?" she asks of His disciples. They give her no information; they had their Master's orders to let Him remain in hiding. He sought quiet, and needed it, and so they discreetly held their tongues. Yet she found Him out, and fell at His feet. Half a hint was dropped; she took up the trail, and followed it until she discovered the house, and sought the Lord in His abode. Here was the beginning of her trial: the Saviour was in hiding. "But He could not be hid" from her eager search; she was all ear and eye for him, and nothing can be hid from an anxious mother, eager to bless her child. Disturbed by her, the Blessed One comes into the street, and His disciples surround Him. She determines to be heard over their heads, and therefore she begins to cry aloud, "Have mercy upon me, O Lord, thou son of David." As He walks along, she still cries out with mighty cries and pleadings, till the streets ring with her voice, and He who "would have no man know it" is proclaimer in the market place. Peter does not like it; he prefers quiet worship. John feels a great deal disturbed by the noise: he lost a sentence just now, a very precious sentence, which the Lord was uttering. The woman's noise was very distracting to everybody, and so the disciples came to Jesus, and they said, "Send her away, send her away; do something for her, or tell her to be gone; for she crieth after us, we have no peace for her clamour; we cannot hear thee speak because of her piteous cries."

Meanwhile, she, perceiving them speaking to Jesus, comes nearer, breaks into the inner circle, falls down before Him, worships Him, and utters this plaintive prayer—"Lord, help me." There is more power in worship than in noise; she has taken a step in advance. Our Lord has not yet answered her a single word. He has heard what she said, no doubt; but He has not answered a word to her as yet. All that He has done is to say to His disciples, "I am not sent but unto the lost sheep of the house of Israel." That has not prevented her nearer approach, or stopped her prayer; for now she pleads, "Lord, help me." At length the Blessed One does speak to her. Greatly to our surprise, it is a chill rebuff. What a cold word it is! How cutting! I dare not say, how cruel! yet it seemed so. "It is not meet to take the children's bread, and to cast it to dogs."

Now, what will the woman do? She is near the Saviour; she has an audience with Him, such as it is; she is on her knees before Him, and He appears to repulse her! How will she act now? Here is the point about which I am going to speak. She will not be repulsed, she perseveres, she advances nearer, she actually turns the rebuff into a plea. She has come for a blessing, and a blessing she believes that she shall have, and she means to plead for it till she wins it. So she deals with the Saviour after a very heroic manner, and in the wisest possible style; from which I want every seeker to learn a lesson at this time, that he, like her, may win with Christ, and hear the Master say to him this morning, "Great is thy faith; be it unto thee even as thou wilt."

Three pieces of advice I gather from this woman's example. First, *agree with the Lord whatever He says.* Say, "Truth, Lord; truth, Lord." Say "Yes" to all His words. Secondly, *plead with the Lord*—"Truth, Lord; yet," "yet." Think of another truth, and mention it to Him as a plea. Say, "Lord, I must maintain my hold; I must plead with Thee yet." And thirdly, *in any case have faith in the Lord, whatever He saith.* However He tries thee, still believe in Him with unstaggering faith, and know of a surety that He deserves thine utmost confidence in His love and power.

I. My first advice to every heart here seeking the Saviour is this, AGREE WITH THE LORD. In the Revised Version we read that she said, "Yea, Lord," or, "Yes, Lord." Whatever Jesus said, she did not contradict Him in the least. I like the old translation, "Truth, Lord," for it is very expressive. She did not say, "It is hard, or unkind"; but "It is true. It is true that it is not meet to take the children's bread, and to cast it to dogs. It is true that compared with Israel I am a dog: for me to gain this blessing would be like a dog's feeding on the children's bread. Truth, Lord; truth, Lord." Now, dear friend, if thou art dealing with the Lord for life and death, *never contradict His word.* Thou wilt never come unto perfect peace if thou art in a contradicting humour; for that is a proud and unacceptable condition of mind. He that reads his Bible to find fault with it will soon discover that the Bible finds fault with him. It may be said of the Book of God as of its Author: "If ye walk contrary to me, I will walk contrary to you." Of this Book I may truly say, "With the froward thou wilt show thyself froward."

Remember, dear friends, that *if the Lord reminds you of your unworthiness and your unfitness, He only tells you what is true,* and it will be your wisdom to say, "Truth, Lord," Scripture describes you as having a depraved nature: say, "Truth, Lord." It describes you as going astray like a lost sheep, and the charge is true. It describes you as having a deceitful heart, and just such a heart you have. Therefore say, "Truth, Lord." It represents you as "without strength," and "without hope." Let your answer be, "Truth, Lord." The Bible never gives unrenewed human nature a good word, nor does it deserve it. It exposes our corruptions, and lays bare our falseness, pride, and unbelief. Cavil not at the faithfulness of the Word. Take the lowest place and own yourself a sinner, lost, ruined, and undone. If the Scripture should seem to degrade you, do not take umbrage thereat, but feel that it deals honestly with you. Never let proud nature contradict the Lord, for this is to increase your sin.

This woman took the very lowest possible place. She not only admitted that she was like one of the little dogs, but she put herself under the table, and under the children's table, rather than under the Master's table. She said, "The dogs eat of the crumbs which fall from their masters' table." Most of you have supposed that she referred to the crumbs that fell from the table of the master of the house himself. If you will kindly look at the passage you will see that it is not so. "Their masters'" refers to several masters: the word is plural, and refers to the children who were the little masters of the little dogs. Thus she humbled herself to be not only as a dog to the Lord, but as a dog to the house of Israel—to the Jews. This was going very far indeed, for a Tyrian woman, of proud Sidonian blood, to admit that the house of Israel were to her as masters, that these disciples who had said just now, "Send her away," stood in the same relation to her as the children of the family stand in towards the little dogs under the table. Great faith is always sister to great humility. It does not matter how low Christ puts her, she sits *there*. "Truth Lord." I earnestly recommend every hearer of mine to consent unto the Lord's verdict, and never to raise an argument against The Sinner's Friend. When thy heart is heavy, when thou hast a sense of being the greatest of sinners, I pray thee remember that thou art a greater sinner than thou thinkest thyself to be. Though conscience has rated thee very low, thou mayest go lower still, and yet be in thy right place; for, truth to tell, thou art as bad as bad can be; thou art worse than thy darkest thoughts have ever painted thee; thou art a wretch most undeserving, and hell-deserving; and apart from sovereign grace thy case is hopeless. It thou wert now in hell, thou wouldst have no cause to complain against the justice of God, for thou deservest to be there. I would to God that every hearer here who has not yet found mercy would consent to the severest declarations of God's Word; for they are all true, and true to him. Oh, that you would say, "Yes, Lord: I have not a syllable to say in self-defence"!

And, next, *if it should appear to your humbled heart to be a very strange thing for you to think of being saved, do not fight against that belief.* If a sense of divine justice should suggest to you—"What! You saved? Then you will be the greatest wonder on earth! What! You saved! Surely, God will have gone beyond all former mercy in pardoning such a one as you are. In that case, He would have taken the children's bread and cast it to a dog. You are so unworthy, and so insignificant and useless, that even if you are saved, you will be good for nothing in holy service." How can you expect the blessing? Do not attempt to argue to the contrary. Seek not to magnify yourself; but cry: "Lord, I agree with Thy valuation of me. I freely admit that if I be forgiven, if I am made a child of God, and if I enter heaven, I shall be the greatest marvel of immeasurable love and boundless grace that ever yet lived in earth or heaven."

We should be the more ready to give our assent and consent to every syllable of the divine word, since *Jesus knows us better than we know ourselves.* The Word of God knows more about us than we can ever discover about ourselves. We are partial to ourselves, and hence we are half blind. Our judgment always fails to hold the balance evenly when our own case is in the weighing. What man is there who is not on good terms with himself? Your faults, of course, are always excusable; and if you do a little good, why, it deserves to be talked of, and to be estimated at the rate of diamonds of the first water. Each one of us is a very superior person; so our proud heart tells us. Our Lord Jesus does not flatter us, He lets us see our case as it is: His searching eye perceives the naked truth of things, and as "the faithful and true Witness" He deals with us after the rule of uprightness. O seeking soul, Jesus loves you too well to flatter you. Therefore, I pray you, have such confidence in Him that, however much He, by His Word and Spirit, may rebuke, reprove, and even condemn you, you may without hesitation reply, "Truth, Lord! Truth, Lord!"

Nothing can be gained by cavilling with the Saviour. A beggar stands at your door and asks for charity: he goes the wrong way to work if he begins a discussion with you, and contradicts your statements. If beggars must not be choosers, certainly they must not be controversialists. If a mendicant will dispute, let him dispute; but let him give up begging. If he cavils as to how he shall receive your gift, or how or what you shall give him, he is likely to be sent about his business. A critical sinner disputing with his Saviour is a fool in capitals. As for me, my mind is made up that I will quarrel with anybody sooner than with my Saviour; and especially I will contend with myself, and pick a desperate quarrel with my own pride, rather than have a shade of difference with my Lord. To contend with one's Benefactor is folly indeed! For the justly condemned to quibble with the Law giver in Whom is vested the prerogative of pardon would be folly. Instead of that, with heart and soul I cry, "Lord, whatever I find in Thy Word, whatever I read in Holy Scripture, which is the revelation of Thy mind, I do believe it, I will believe it, I must believe it; and I, therefore, say, 'Truth, Lord!' It is all true, though it condemn me, for ever."

Now, mark this: if you find your heart agreeing with what Jesus says, even when He answers you roughly, you may depend upon it *this is a work of grace ;* for human nature is very upstart, and stands very much upon its silly dignity, and therefore it contradicts the Lord, when He deals truthfully with it, and humbles it. Human nature, if you want to see it in its true condition, is that naked thing over yonder, which so proudly aims at covering itself with a dress of its own devising. See, it sews fig leaves together to make itself an apron! What a destitute object! With its withered leaves about it, it seems worse than naked! Yet this wretched human nature proudly rebels against salvation by Christ. It will not hear of imputed righteousness: its own righteousness is dearer far. Woe be to the crown of pride which rivals the Lord Christ! If, my hearer, thou art of another mind, and art willing to own thyself a sinner, lost, ruined, and condemned, it is well with thee. If thou art of this mind, that whatever humbling truth the Spirit of God may teach thee in the Word, or teach by the conviction of thy conscience, thou wilt at once agree therewith, and confess, "It is even so"; then the Spirit of God has brought thee to this humble and truthful and obedient condition, and things are going hopefully with thee.

II. And now my second point is this: although you must not cavil with Christ, you may PLEAD WITH Him. "Truth, Lord," she says; but she adds, "yet."

Here, then, is my first lesson: *set one truth over against another.* Do not contradict a frowning truth, but bring up a smiling one to meet it. Remember how the Jews were saved out of the hands of their enemies in the days of Haman and Mordecai. The king issued a decree that, on a certain day, the people might rise up against the Jews, and slay them, and take their possessions as a spoil. Now, according to the laws of the Medes and Persians, this could not be altered: the decree must stand. What then? How was it to be got over? Why, by meeting that ordinance by another. Another decree is issued, that although the people might rise against the Jews, yet the Jews might defend themselves;

and if anybody dared to hurt them, they might slay them, and take their property to be a prey. One decree thus counteracted another.

How often we may use the holy art of looking from one doctrine to another! If a truth looks black upon me, I shall not be wise to be always dwelling upon it; but it will be my wisdom to examine the whole range of truth, and see if there be not some other doctrine which will give me hope. David practised this when he said of himself, "So foolish was I, and ignorant: I was as a beast before thee." And then he most confidently added, "Nevertheless I am continually with thee: thou hast holden me by my right hand." He does not contradict himself, and yet the second utterance removes all the bitterness which the first sentence left upon the palate. The two sentences together set forth the supreme grace of God, who enabled a poor beast-like being to commune with himself. I beg you to learn this holy art of setting one truth side by side with another, that thus you may have a fair view of the whole situation, and may not despair.

For instance, I meet with men who say, "O sir, sin is an awful thing; it condemns me. I feel I can never answer the Lord for my iniquities, nor stand in His holy presence." This is assuredly true; but remember another truth: "The Lord hath laid on him the iniquity of us all "; "He was made sin for us, who knew no sin"; "There is therefore now no condemnation to them which are in Christ Jesus." Set the truth of the sin-bearing of our Lord over against the guilt and curse of sin due to yourself apart from your great Substitute.

"The Lord has an elect people," cries one, "and this discourages me." Why should it? Do not contradict that truth; believe it as you read it in God's Word: but hear how Jesus puts it: "I thank thee, O Father, Lord of heaven and earth, because thou hast hid these things from the wise and prudent, and hast revealed them unto babes." To you who are weak, simple, and trustful as babes, the doctrine is full of comfort. If the Lord will save a number that no man can number, why should He not save me? It is true it is written, "All that the Father giveth me shall come to me"; but it is also written, "And him that cometh to me I will in no wise cast out." Let the second half of the saying be accepted as well as the first half.

Some are stumbled by the sovereignty of God. He will have mercy on whom He will have mercy. He may justly ask, "Shall I not do as I will with my own?" Beloved, do not dispute the rights of the eternal God. It is the Lord: let Him do as seemeth Him good. Do not quarrel with the King; but come humbly to Him, and plead thus: "O Lord, thou alone hast the right to pardon; but then thy Word declares that if we confess our sins, thou art faithful and just to forgive us our sins; and thou hast said, that whosoever believeth in the Lord Jesus Christ shall be saved." This pleading will prevail. When thou readest, "Ye must be born again," do not be angry. It is true that to be born again is a work beyond thy power: it is the work of the Holy Spirit; and this need of a work beyond thy reach may well distress thee. But that third chapter of John, which says, "Ye must be born again," also says, "God so loved the world, that he gave his only-begotten Son, that whosoever believeth in him should not perish, but have everlasting life." Thus, it is clear that he that believeth in Jesus is born again.

This brings me to a second remark: *draw comfort even from a hard truth.* Take this advice in preference to that which I have already given. The Authorized translation here is very good, but I must confess that it is not quite so true to the woman's meaning as the Revised Version. She did not say, "Truth, Lord: *yet,*" as if she were raising an objection, as I have already put it to you; but she said, "Truth, Lord, for." I have gone with the old translation, because it expresses the way in which our mind too generally looks at things. We fancy that we set one truth over against another, whereas all truths are agreed, and cannot be in conflict. Out of the very truth which looks darkest we may gain consolation. She said, "Yes, Lord; for the dogs eat the crumbs which fall from their masters' table." She did not draw comfort from another truth which seemed to neutralize the first; but, as the bee sucks honey from the nettle, so did she gather encouragement from the severe Word of the Lord—"It is not meet to take the children's bread, and to cast it to dogs." She said, "That is true, Lord, for even the dogs eat the crumbs that fall from their master's table." She had not to turn what Christ said upside down; she took it as it stood, and spied out comfort in it. Earnestly would I urge you to learn the art of deriving comfort from every statement of God's Word; not necessarily bringing up a second doctrine, but believing that even the present truth which bears a threatening aspect is yet your friend.

Do I hear you say, "How can I have hope? for salvation is of the Lord." Why, that is the very reason why you should be filled with hope, and seek salvation of the Lord alone. If it were of yourself, you might despair; but as it is of the Lord, you may have hope.

Do you groan out, "Alas! I can do nothing"? What of that? The Lord can do everything. Since salvation is of the Lord alone, ask Him to be its Alpha and Omega to you. Do you groan,

"I know I must repent; but I am so unfeeling that I cannot reach the right measure of tenderness." This is true, and therefore the Lord Jesus is exalted on high to give repentance. You will no more repent in your own power than you will go to heaven in your own merit; but the Lord will grant you repentance unto life; for this, also, is a fruit of the Spirit.

Beloved, when I was under a sense of sin I heard the doctrine of divine sovereignty, "He will have mercy on whom he will have mercy"; but that did not frighten me at all; for I felt more hopeful of grace through the sovereign will of God than by any other way. If pardon be not a matter of human deserving, but of divine prerogative, then there is hope for me. Why should not I be forgiven as well as others? If the Lord had only three elect ones, and these were chosen according to His own good pleasure, why should not I be one of them? I laid myself at His feet, and gave up every hope but that which flowed from His mercy. Knowing that He would save a number that no man could number, and that He would save every soul that believed in Jesus, I believed and was saved. It was well for me that salvation did not turn upon merit; for I had no merit whatever. If it remained with sovereign grace, then I also could go through that door; for the Lord might as well save me as any other sinner; and inasmuch as I read, "Him that cometh to me I will in no wise cast out," I even came, and He did not cast me out.

Rightly understood, every truth in God's word leads to Jesus, and no single word drives the seeking sinner back. If thou be a fine fellow, full of thine own righteousness, every gospel truth looks black on thee; but if thou be a sinner deserving nothing of God but wrath—if in thy heart thou dost confess that thou deservest condemnation, thou art the kind of man that Christ came to save, thou art the sort of man that God chose from before the foundation of the world, and thou mayest, without any hesitancy, come and put thy trust in Jesus, who is the sinner's Saviour. Believing in Him, thou shalt receive immediate salvation.

III. Thirdly, in any case, whatever Christ saith or doth not say, HAVE THOU FAITH IN HIM. Look at this woman's faith and try to copy it. It grew in its apprehension of Jesus.

First, He is *the Lord of mercy* : she cried, "Have mercy on me." Have faith enough, dear hearer, to believe that thou needest mercy. Mercy is not for the meritorious: the claim of the meritorious is for justice, not for mercy. The guilty need and seek mercy; and only they. Believe that God delighteth in mercy, delighteth to give grace where it cannot be deserved, delighteth to forgive where there is no reason for forgiveness but His own goodness.   Believe also that the Lord Jesus Christ whom we preach to you is the incarnation of mercy: His very existence is mercy to you, His every word means mercy; His life, His death, His intercession in heaven, all mean mercy, mercy, mercy, nothing but mercy. You need divine mercy, and Jesus is the embodiment of divine mercy—He is the Saviour for you. Believe in Him, and the mercy of God is yours.

This woman also called Him *Son of David*, in which she recognized His manhood and His kingship towards man. I think of Jesus Christ as God over all, blessed for ever, He that made the heaven and the earth, and upholdeth all things by the word of His power. Know that He became man, veiling His Godhead in this poor clay of ours: He hung as a babe upon a woman's breast, He sat as a weary man upon the curb of a well, He died with malefactors on the cross; and all this out of love to man. Can you not trust this Son of David? David was very popular because he went in and out amongst the people, and proved himself the people's king. Jesus is such. David gathered to him a company of men who were greatly attached to him, because when they came to him they were a broken-down crew; they were in debt, and discontented; all the outcasts from Saul's dominions came around David, and he became a captain to them.

My Lord Jesus Christ is one chosen out of the people, chosen by God on purpose to be a brother to us, a brother born for adversity, a brother who has come to associate with us, despite our meanness and misery. He is the friend of men and women who are ruined by their guilt and sin. "This man receiveth sinners, and eateth with them." Jesus is the willing leader of a people sinful and defiled, whom He raises to justification and holiness, and makes to dwell with Himself in glory for ever. Oh, will you not trust such a Saviour as this? My Lord did not come into the world to save superior people, who think themselves born saints. But Jesus came to save the lost, the ruined, the guilty, the unworthy. Let such come clustering round Him like the bees around the queen bee, for He is ordained on purpose to collect the Lord's chosen ones, as it is written, "Unto him shall the gathering of the people be."

This believing woman might have been cheered by another theme. Our Lord said to His disciples, "I am not sent but unto the lost sheep of the house of Israel." "Ah!" thinks she, "He is a Shepherd for lost sheep. Whatever His flock may be, *He is a shepherd*, and He has bowels of compassion for poor lost sheep: surely He is one to whom I may look with confidence." Ah, dear hearer! my Lord Jesus Christ is a shepherd by office and by nature, and if you are a lost sheep this is good tidings for you. There is a holy instinct in Him which makes Him gather the lambs with His arms, and causes Him to search out the lost ones, who were scattered in the cloudy and dark day. Trust Him to seek you; yea, come to Him now, and leave yourselves with Him.

Father than that, this woman had a faith in Christ that He was like *a great householder*. She seems to say, "Those disciples are children who sit at table, and He feeds them on the bread of His love. He makes for them so great a feast, and He gives to them so much food, that if my daughter were healed, it would be a great and blessed thing to me, but to Him it would be no more than if a crumb fell under the table, and a dog fed thereon." She does not ask to have a crumb thrown to her, but only to be allowed to pick up a crumb that has fallen from the table. She asks not even for a crumb which the Lord may drop; but for one which the children have let fall: they are generally great crumb-makers. I notice in the Greek, that as the word for "dogs," is "little dogs"; so the word rendered "crumbs" is "little crumbs"—small, inconsidered morsels, which fall by accident. Think of this faith. To have the devil cast out of her daughter was the greatest thing she could imagine; and yet she had such a belief in the greatness of the Lord Christ, that she thought it would be no more to Him to make her daughter well than for a great housekeeper to let a poor little dog eat a tiny crumb that had been dropped by a child. Is not that splendid faith?

And now, canst thou exercise such a faith? Canst thou believe it—thou, a condemned, lost sinner—that if God save thee it will be the greatest wonder that ever was; and yet that to Jesus, who made Himself a sacrifice for sin, it will be no more than if this day thy dog or thy cat should eat a tiny morsel that one of thy children had dropped from the table? Canst thou think Jesus to be so great, that what is heaven to thee will be only a crumb to Him? Canst thou believe that He can save thee readily? As for me, I believe my Lord to be such a Saviour that I can trust my soul wholly to Him, and that without difficulty. And I will tell you something else: if I had all your souls in my body, I would trust them all to Jesus. Yea, and if I had a million sinful souls of my own, I would freely trust the Lord Christ with the whole of them, and I would say, "I am persuaded that He is able to keep that which I have committed to Him against that day."

Do not suppose that I speak thus because I am conscious of any goodness of my own. Far from it: my trust is in no degree in myself, or anything I can do or be. If I were good I could not trust in Jesus. Why should I? I should trust myself. But because I have nothing of my own, I am obliged to live by trust, and I am rejoiced that I may do so. My Lord gives me unlimited credit at the Bank of Faith. I am very deeply in debt to Him, and I am resolved to be more indebted still. Sinner as I am, if I were a million times as sinful as I am, and then had a million souls each one a million times more sinful than my own, I would still trust His atoning blood to cleanse me, and Himself to save me. By Thine agony and bloody sweat, by Thy cross and passion, by Thy precious death and burial, by Thy glorious resurrection and ascension, by Thine intercession for the guilty at the right hand of God, O Christ, I feel that I can repose in Thee. May you come to this point, all of you; that Jesus is abundantly able to save.

You have been a thief, have you? The last person that was in our Lord's near company on earth was the dying thief. "Oh!" but you say, "I have been foul in life; I have defiled myself with all manner of evil." But those with whom He associates now were all of them once unclean; for they confess that they have washed their robes, and made them white in His blood. Their robes were once so foul that nothing but His heart's blood could have made them white. Jesus is a great Saviour, greater than my tongue can tell. I fail to speak His worth, and I should still fail to do so, even if I could speak heaven in every word, and express infinity in every sentence. Not all the tongues of men or of angels can fully set forth the greatness of the grace of our Redeemer. Trust Him! Are you afraid to trust Him? Then make a dash for it. Venture to do so.

"Venture on him, venture wholly; Let no other trust intrude."

"Look unto me," saith he, "and be ye saved, all the ends of the earth: for I am God, and there is none else." Look! Look now! Look to Him alone; and as you look to Him with the look of faith He will look on you with loving acceptance, and say, "Great is thy faith: be it unto thee even as thou wilt." Thou shalt be saved at this very hour; and though thou camest into this house of prayer grievously vexed with a devil, thou shalt go out at peace with God, and as restful as an angel. God grant thee this boon, for Christ's sake. Amen.

K

DAVID'S PRAYER IN THE CAVE

A SERMON

Text.—"Maschil of David; A Prayer when he was in the cave."
—Title of Psalm cxlii.

"A PRAYER when he was in the cave." David did pray when he was in the cave. If he had prayed half as much when he was in the palace as he did when he was in the cave, it would have been better for him. But, alas! when he was king, we find him rising from his bed in the evening, and looking from the roof of the house, and falling into temptation. If he had been looking up to heaven, if his heart had been in communion with God, he might never have committed that great crime which has so deeply stained his whole character.

"A prayer when he was in the cave." God will hear prayer on the land, and on the sea, and even under the sea. I remember a brother, when in prayer, making use of that last expression. Somebody who was at the prayer-meeting was rather astonished at it, and asked, "How would God hear prayer under the sea?" On enquiry, we found out that the man who uttered those words was a diver, and often went down to the bottom of the sea after wrecks; and he said that he had held communion with God while he had been at work in the depths of the ocean. Our God is not the God of the hills only; but of the valleys also; He is God of both sea and land. He heard Jonah when the disobedient prophet was at the bottom of the mountains, and the earth with her bars seemed to be about him for ever. Wherever you work, you can pray. Wherever you lie sick, you can pray. There is no place to which you can be banished where God is not near, and there is no time of day or night when His throne is inaccessible.

"A prayer when he was in the cave." The caves have heard the best prayers. Some birds sing best in cages. I have heard that some of God's people shine brightest in the dark. There is many an heir of heaven who never prays so well as when he is driven by necessity to pray. Some shall sing aloud upon their beds of sickness, whose voices were hardly heard when they were well; and some shall sing God's high praises in the fire, who did not praise Him as they should before the trial came. In the furnace of affliction the saints are often seen at their best. If any of you to-night are in dark and gloomy positions, if your souls are bowed down within you, may this become a special time for peculiarly prevalent communion and intercession, and may the prayer of the cave be the very best of your prayers!

I shall, to-night, use David's prayer in the cave to represent the prayers of godly men in trouble; but, first, I will talk of it as a picture of *the condition of a soul under a deep sense of sin.* This Psalm of the cave has a great likeness to the character of a man under a sense of sin. I shall then use it to represent *the condition of a persecuted believer ;* and, thirdly, I shall speak of it as revealing *the condition of a believer who is being prepared for greater honour and wider service* than he has ever attained before.

I. First, let me try and use this Psalm as a picture of THE CONDITION OF A SOUL UNDER A DEEP SENSE OF SIN.

A little while ago, you were out in the open field of the world, sinning with a high hand, plucking the flowers which grow in those poisoned vales, and enjoying their deadly perfume. You were as happy as your sinful heart could be; for you were giddy and careless, and thoughtless; but it has pleased God to arrest you. You have been apprehended by Christ, and you have been put in prison, and now your feet are fast in the stocks. To-night, you feel like one who has come out of the bright sunshine and balmy air into a dark, noisome cavern, where you can see but little, where there is no comfort, and where there appears to you to be no hope of escape.

Well, now, according to the Psalm before us, which is meant for you as well as for David, your first business should be to *appeal unto God.* I know your doubts; I know your fears of God; I know how frightened you are at the very mention of His name; but I charge you, if you would come out of your present gloom, go to God at once. See, the Psalm begins, "I cried unto the Lord with my voice; with my voice unto the Lord did I make my supplication." Get home, and cry to God with your voice; but if you have no place where you can use your voice, cry to God in silence; but do cry to Him. Look God-ward; if you look any other way, all is darkness. Look God-ward; there, and there only, is hope.

"But I have sinned against God," say you. But God is ready to pardon; He has provided a great atonement, through which He can justly forgive the greatest offences. Look God-ward, and begin to pray. I have known men, who have hardly believed in God, do this; but they have had some faint desire to do so, and they have cried; it has been a poor prayer, and yet God has heard it. I have known some cry to God in very despair. When they hardly believed that there could be any use in it, still it was that or nothing; and they knew that it could not hurt them to pray, and so they took to their knees, and they cried. It is wonderful what poor prayers God will hear, and answer, too; prayers that have no legs to run with, and no hands to grasp with, and very little heart; but still, God has heard them, and He has accepted them. Get to your knees, you who feel yourselves guilty; get to your knees, if your hearts are sighing on account of sin. If the dark gloom of your iniquities is gathering about you, cry to God; and He will hear you.

The next thing to do is, *make a full confession*. David says, "I poured out my complaint before him; I shewed before him my trouble." The human heart longs to express itself; an unuttered grief will lie and smoulder in the soul, till its black smoke puts out the very eyes of the spirit. It is not a bad thing sometimes to speak to some Christian friend about the anguish of your heart. I would not encourage you to put that in the first place; far from it; but still it may be helpful to some. But, anyhow, make a full confession unto the Lord. Tell Him how you have sinned; tell Him how you have tried to save yourself, and broken down; tell Him what a wretch you are, how changeable, how fickle, how proud, how wanton, how your ambition carries you away like an unbridled steed. Tell Him all your faults, as far as you can remember them; do not attempt to hide anything from God; you cannot do so, for He knows all; therefore, hesitate not to tell Him everything, the darkest secret, the sin you would not wish even to whisper to the evening's gale. Tell it all; tell it all. Confession to God is good for the soul. "Whoso confesseth and forsaketh his sins shall have mercy."

I do press upon any of you who are now in the gloomy cave, that you seek a secret and quiet place, and, alone with God, pour out your heart before Him. David says, "I shewed before him my trouble." Do not think that the use of pious words can be of any avail; it is not merely words that you have to utter, you have to lay all your trouble before God. As a child tells its mother its griefs, tell the Lord all your griefs, your complaints, your miseries, your fears. Tell them all out, and great relief will come to your spirit. So, first, appeal to God. Secondly, make confession to Him.

Thirdly, *acknowledge to God that there is no hope for you but in His mercy*. Put it as David did, "I looked on my right hand, and behold, but there was no man that would know me." There is but one hope for you; acknowledge that. Perhaps you have been trying to be saved by your good works. They are altogether worthless when you heap them together. Possibly you expect to be saved by your religiousness. Half of it is hypocrisy; and how can a man hope to be saved by his hypocrisy? Do you hope

to be saved by your feelings? What are your feelings? As changeable as the weather; a puff of wind will change all your fine
feelings into murmuring and rebellion against God. Oh, friend,
you cannot keep the law of God! That is the only other way to
heaven. The perfect keeping of God's commandments would
save you if you had never committed a sin; but, having sinned,
even that will not save you now, for future obedience will not
wipe out past disobedience. Here, in Christ Jesus, whom God
sets forth as a propitiation for sin, is the only hope for you; lay
hold on it. In the cave of your doubts and fears, with the clinging
damp of your despair about you, chilled and numbed by the
dread of the wrath to come, yet venture to make God in Christ
your sole confidence, and you shall yet have perfect peace.

Then, further, if you are still in the cave of doubt and sin,
venture to *plead with God to set you free.* You cannot present a
better prayer than this one of David in the cave, "Bring my soul
out of prison, that I may praise thy name." You are in prison
to-night, and you cannot get out of it by yourself. You may get
a hold of those bars, and try to shake them to and fro, but they
are fast in their sockets; they will not break in your hands.
You may meditate, and think, and invent, and excogitate;
but you cannot open that great iron gate; but there is a hand that
can break gates of brass, and there is a power that can cut in sunder
bars of iron. O man in the iron cage, there is a hand that can
crumble up thy cage, and set thee free! Thou needest not be
a prisoner; thou needest not be shut up; thou mayest walk at
large through Jesus Christ the Saviour. Only trust Him, and
believingly pray that prayer to-night, "Bring my soul out of prison,
that I may praise thy name," and He will set you free. Ah,
sinners do praise God's name when they get out of prison! I
recollect how, when I was set free, I felt like singing all the
time, and I could quite well use the language of Charles Wesley,—

> " Oh, for a thousand tongues to sing
>   My great Redeemer's praise!"

My old friend, Dr. Alexander Fletcher, seems to rise before me
now, for I remember hearing him say to the children that, when
men came out of prison, they did praise him who had set them
free. He said that he was going down the Old Bailey one day,
and he saw a boy standing on his head, turning Catherine wheels,
dancing hornpipes, and jumping about in all manner of ways,
and he said to him, "What are you at? You seem to be tremend-
ously happy"; and the boy replied, "Ah, old gentleman, if
you had been locked up six months, and had just got out, you

would be happy, too!" I have no doubt that is very true. When a soul gets out of a far worse prison than there ever was at Newgate, then he must praise "free grace and dying love," and "ring those charming bells," again, and again, and again, and make his whole life musical with the praise of the emancipating Christ.

Now, that is my advice to you who are in the cave through soul-trouble. May God bless it to you! You need not notice anything else that I am going to say to-night. If you are under a sense of sin, heed well what I have been saying; and let other people have the rest of the sermon that belongs more especially to them.

II. I pass on to my second point. This Psalm may well help to set forth THE CONDITION OF A PERSECUTED BELIEVER.

A persecuted believer! Are there any such nowadays? Ah, dear friends, there are many such! When a man becomes a Christian, he straightway becomes different from the rest of his fellows. When I lived in a street, I was standing one day at the window, meditating what my sermon should be, and I could not find a text, when, all of a sudden, I saw a flight of birds. There was a canary, which had escaped from its cage, and was flying over the slates of the opposite houses, and it was being chased by some twenty sparrows, and other rough birds. Then I thought of that text, "My heritage is unto me as a speckled bird; the birds round about are against her." Why, they seemed to say to one another, "Here is a yellow fellow; we have not seen the like of him in London; he has no business here; let us pull off his bright coat, let us kill him, or make him as dark and dull as ourselves." That is just what men of the world try to do with Christians. Here is a godly man who works in a factory, or a Christian girl who is occupied in book-folding, or some other work where there is a large number employed; such persons will have a sad tale to tell of how they have been hunted about, ridiculed, and scoffed at by ungodly companions. Now you are in the cave.

It may be that you are in the condition described here; *you hardly know what to do.* You are as David was when he wrote the third verse, "When my spirit was overwhelmed within me." The persecutors have so turned against you, and it is so new a thing to you as a young believer, that you are quite perplexed, and hard put to it to know what you should do. They are so severe, they are so ferocious, they are so incessant, and they find out your tender points, and they know how to touch you just on the raw places; that you really do not know what to do. You are like a lamb in the midst of wolves; you know not which way to turn. Well, then, say to the Lord, as David did, "When my spirit was overwhelmed within me, then thou knewest my path." God knows exactly where you are, and what you have to bear. Have confidence that, when you know not what to do, He can and will direct your way if you trust Him.

In addition to that, it may be that *you are greatly tempted*. David said, "They privily laid a snare for me." It is often so with young men in a warehouse, or with a number of clerks in an establishment. They find that a young fellow has become a Christian, and they try to trip him up. If they can, they will get up some scheme by which they can make him appear to have been guilty, even if he has not. Ah, you will want much wisdom! I pray God that you may never yield to temptation; but may hold your ground by divine grace. Young Christian soldiers often have a very rough time of it in the barracks; but I hope that they will prove themselves true soldiers, and not yield an inch to those who would lead them astray.

It will be very painful if, in addition to that, *your friends turn against you*. David said, "There was no man that would know me." Is it so with you? Are your father and mother against you? Is your wife or your husband against you? Do your brothers and sisters call you "a canting hypocrite?" Do they point the finger of scorn at you when you get home? And often, when you go from the Lord's table, where you have been so happy, do you have to hear an oath the first thing when you enter the door? I know that it is so with many of you. The Church of Christ in London is like Lot in Sodom; they who look for brighter times must be looking with their eyes shut. There is grave occasion for Christians to pray for young people who are converted in such a city as this, for their worst enemies are often those of their own household. "I should not mind so much," says one, "if I had a Christian friend to fly to. I spoke to one the other day, and he did not seem to interest himself in me at all."

I will tell you what hurts a young convert. Here is one just saved; he has really, lovingly, given his heart to Christ, and the principal or manager where he works is a Christian man. He finds himself ridiculed, and he ventures to say a word to this Christian man. He snuffs him out in a moment, he has no sympathy with him. Well, there is another old professing Christian working near at the same bench; and the young convert begins to tell him a little about his trouble, and he is very grumpy and cross. I have noticed some Christian people who appear to be shut up in themselves, and they do not seem to notice the troubles of beginners in the divine life. Let it not be so among you. My dear brothers and sisters, cultivate great love to those who, having come into the army of Christ, are much beset by adversaries.

They are in the cave. Do not disown them; they are trying to do their best; stand side by side with them. Say, "I, too, am a Christian. If you are honouring that young man with your ridicule, let me have my portion of it. If you are pouring contempt upon him, give me a share of it, for I also believe as he believes."

Will you do that? Some of you will, I am sure. Will you stand by the man of God who vindicates the Lord's revealed truth? Some of you will; but there are plenty of fellows who want to keep a whole skin on their body, and if they can sneak away out of any fight for the right, they are glad to get home and go to bed, and there slumber till the battle is over. God help us to have more of the lion in us, and not so much of the cur! God grant us grace to stand by those who are out and out for God, and for His Christ, that we may be remembered with them in the day of His appearing!

It may be that the worst point about you is that *you feel very feeble*. You say, "I should not mind the persecution if I felt strong; but I am so feeble." Well, now, always distinguish between feeling strong and being strong. The man who feels strong is weak; the man who feels weak is the man who is strong. Paul said, "When I am weak, then am I strong." David prays, "Deliver me from my persecutors; for they are stronger than I." Just hide yourself away in the strength of God; pray much; take God for your refuge and your portion; have faith in Him; and you will be stronger than your adversaries. They may seem to pull you over; but you will soon be up again. They may set before you puzzles that you cannot solve; they may come up with their scientific knowledge; and you may be at a discount: but never mind that; the God Who has led you into the cave will turn the tables for you one of these days. Only hold on, and hold out, even to the end.

I am rather glad that there should be some trouble in being a Christian, for it has become such a very general thing now to profess to be one. If I am right, it is going to be a very much less common thing than it is now for a man to say, "I am a Christian." There will come times when there will be sharp lines drawn. Some of us will help to draw them if we can, when men shall bear the Christian name, and then act like worldlings, and love the amusements and the follies of worldlings. It is time that there was a division in the house of the Lord, and that the "ayes" went into one lobby, and the "noes" into the other lobby. We have too long been mixed together; and I for one say, may the day soon come when every Christian will have to run the gauntlet! It will be a good thing for genuine believers.

It will just blow some of the chaff away from the wheat. We shall have all the purer gold when the fire gets hot, and the crucible is put into it, for then the dross will be separated from the precious metal. Be of good courage, my brother, if thou art now in the cave, the Lord will bring thee out of it in His own good time!

III. Now, to close, I want to speak a little about THE CONDITION OF A BELIEVER WHO IS BEING PREPARED FOR GREATER HONOUR AND WIDER SERVICE.

Is it not a curious thing that, whenever God means to make a man great, He always breaks him in pieces first? There was a man whom the Lord meant to make into a prince. How did He do it? Why, He met him one night, and wrestled with him! You always hear about Jacob's wrestling. Well, I dare say he did; but it was not Jacob who was the principal wrestler: "There wrestled a man with him until the breaking of the day." God touched the hollow of Jacob's thigh, and put it out of joint, before He called him "Israel"; that is, "a prince of God." The wrestling was to take all his strength out of him; and when his strength was gone, then God called him a prince. Now, David was to be king over all Israel. What was the way to Jerusalem for David? What was the way to the throne? Well, it was round by the cave of Adullam. He must go there, and be an outlaw, and an outcast, for that was the way by which he would be made king.

Have none of you ever noticed, in your own lives, that whenever God is going to give you an enlargement, and bring you out to a larger sphere of service, or a higher platform of spiritual life, you always get thrown down? That is His usual way of working; He makes you hungry before He feeds you; He strips you before He robes you; He makes nothing of you before He makes something of you. This was the way with David. He is to be king in Jerusalem; but he must go to the throne by the way of the cave. Now, are any of you here going to heaven, or going to a more heavenly state of sanctification, or going to a greater sphere of usefulness? Do not wonder if you go by the way of the cave. Why is that?

It is, first, because, if God would make you greatly useful, He must *teach you how to pray*. The man who is a great preacher, and yet cannot pray, will come to a bad end. A woman who cannot pray, and yet is noted for the conducting of Bible-classes, has already come to a bad end. If you can be great without prayer, your greatness will be your ruin. If God means to bless you greatly, He will make you pray greatly, as He does David who says in this part of his preparation for coming to his throne, "I cried unto the Lord with my voice: with my voice unto the Lord did I make my supplication."

Next, the man whom God would greatly honour must *always believe in God when he is at his wits' end.* "When my spirit was overwhelmed within me, then thou knewest my path." Are you never at your wits' end? Then God has not sent you to do business in great waters; for, if he has, you will reel to and fro, and be at your wits' end, in a great storm, before long. Oh, it is easy ,to trust when you can trust yourself; but when you cannot trust yourself, when you are dead beat, when your spirit sinks below zero in the chill of utter despair, then is the time to trust in God. If that is your case, you have the marks of a man who can lead God's people, and be a comforter of others.

Next, in order to greater usefulnes, many a man of God must be taught *to stand quite alone.* "I looked on my right hand, and behold, but there was no man that would know me." If you want men to help you, you may make a very decent follower; but if you want no man, and can stand alone, God being your Helper, you shall be helped to be a leader. Oh, it was a grand thing when Luther stepped out from the ranks of Rome. There were many good men round him, who said, "Be quiet, Martin. You will get burnt if you do not hold your tongue. Let us keep where we are, in the Church of Rome, even if we have to swallow down great lumps of dirt. We can believe the gospel, and still remain where we are." But Luther knew that he must defy Anti-Christ, and declare the pure gospel of the blessed God; and he must stand alone for the truth, even if there were as many devils against him as there were tiles on the housetops at Worms. That is the kind of man whom God blesses. I would to God that many a young man here might have the courage to feel, in his particular position, "I can stand alone, if need be. I am glad to have my master and my fellow-workmen with me; but if nobody will go to heaven with me, I will say farewell to them, and go to heaven alone through the grace of God's dear Son."

Once more, the man whom God will bless must be the man who *delights in God alone.* David says, "I cried unto thee, O Lord: I said, thou art my refuge and my portion in the land of the living." Oh, to have God as our refuge, and to make God our portion! "You will lose your situation; you will lose your income; you will lose the approbation of your fellow-men." "Ah!" says the believer, "but I shall not lose my portion, for God is my portion. He is situation, and income, and everything to me; and I will hold by Him, come what may." If thou hast learnt to "delight thyself in the Lord, He will give thee the desires of thine heart." Now thou art come into such a state that God can use thee, and make much of thee; but until thou dost make much of God, He never will make much of thee. God deliver us from having our portion in this life, for, if we have, we are not among His people at all!

He whom God would use must be taught *sympathy with God's poor people.* Hence we get these words of David, in the sixth verse, "I am brought very low." Mr. Greatheart, though he must be strong to kill Giant Grim, and any others of the giants that infest the pilgrim path, must be a man who has gone that road himself, if he is to be a leader of others. If the Lord can and is to bless you, my brother, and to make you very useful in His church, depend upon it He will try you. Half, perhaps nine-tenths, of the trials of God's ministers are not sent to them on their own account; but they are sent for the good of other people. Many a child of God, who goes very smoothly to heaven, does very little for others; but another of the Lord's children, who has all the ins and outs and changes of an experienced believer's life has them only that he may be the better fitted to help others; to sit down and weep with them that weep, or to stand up and rejoice with them that rejoice.

So then you, dear brethren, who have got into the cave, and you, my sisters, who have deep spiritual exercises, I want to comfort you by showing you that this is God's way of making something of you. He is digging you out; you are like an old ditch, you cannot hold any more, and God is digging you out to make more room for more grace. That spade will cut sharply, and dig up sod after sod, and throw it on one side. The very thing you would like to keep shall be cast away, and you shall be hollowed out, and dug out, that the word of Elisha may be fulfilled, "Make this valley full of ditches. For thus saith the Lord, Ye shall not see wind, neither shall ye see rain; yet that valley shall be filled with water." You are to be tried, my friend, that God may be glorified in you.

Lastly, if God means to use you, you must get to be *full of praise.* Listen to what David says, "Bring my soul out of prison, that I may praise thy name: the righteous shall compass me about; for thou shalt deal bountifully with me." May God give to my brothers and sisters here, who are just about being tried for their good, and afflicted for their promotion, grace to begin to praise Him! It is the singers that go before; they that can praise best shall be fit to lead others in the work. Do not set me to follow a gloomy leader. Oh, no, dear sirs, we cannot work to the tune of "The Dead March in *Saul*"! Our soldiers would never have won Waterloo if that had been the music for the day of battle. No, no; give us a *Jubilate :* "Sing unto the Lord who hath triumphed gloriously; praise His great name again and again." Then draw the sword, and strike home. If thou art of a cheerful spirit, glad in the Lord, and joyous after all thy trials and afflictions, and if thou dost but rejoice the more because thou hast been brought so low, then God is making something of thee, and He will yet use thee to lead His people to greater works of grace.

I have just talked to three kinds of people to-night. May God grant each of you grace to take what belongs to you! But if you see any of the first sort before you go out of the building, any who are in the cave of gloom under a sense of sin, if you want to go to the communion, but feel that you ought to stop and comfort them, mind that you do the latter. Put yourself second. There is a wonderful work to be done in those lobbies, and in those pews, after a service. There are some dear brethren and sisters who are always doing it; they call themselves my "dogs"; for they go and pick up the birds that I have wounded. I wish that they might be able to pick up many to-night. Oh, that some of you might always be on the alert to watch a face, and see whether there is any emotion there! Just paddle your own canoe alongside that little ship, and see whether you cannot get into communication with the poor troubled one on board, and say a word to cheer a sad heart. Always be doing this; for if you are in prison yourself the way out of it is to help another out. God turned the captivity of Job when he prayed for his friends. When we begin to look after others, and seek to help others, God will bless us. So may it be, for His name's sake! Amen.